NURSULTAN
NAZARBAYEV

NURSULTAN

NAZARBAYEV

MY LIFE, MY TIMES
AND THE FUTURE ...

Translated and Edited by
PETER CONRADI

PILKINGTON PRESS

PUBLISHED IN ENGLISH TRANSLATION 1998
BY PILKINGTON PRESS LTD
YELVERTOFT MANOR
NORTHAMPTONSHIRE NN6 6LF

ISBN 1 899044 19 1

PRODUCED, DESIGNED AND TYPESET BY
A.H. JOLLY (EDITORIAL) LTD
YELVERTOFT MANOR
NORTHAMPTONSHIRE NN6 6LF

PRINTED BY
CLIFFORD PRESS LTD, COVENTRY

CONTENTS

INTRODUCTION

IT MAY be unusual, but this book was written by chance. I was approached by a publishing house to write my autobiography for a political encyclopaedia. They felt that information about the President of Kazakhstan should only come from me.

I cannot say that I warmed to the idea of writing an autobiography because of the lack of time. I wrote this book in odd moments, sometimes helped by assistants who wrote from my dictation. Soon I came to realise that I enjoyed writing this book – one fact reminding me of another, and one memory crossing another. I finally finished my autobiography, which was exactly what the publishers had asked me to do, but I found I was still working on some chapters some months later.

I was told that Beethoven's biographer first called his book 'Only Beethoven', later he changed the subject to 'Beethoven and Myself', then 'I and Beethoven' and finally to 'Only Myself'.

I was the opposite. I began writing about myself and finished talking about my friends and colleagues and about Kazakhstan and its people.

I must especially thank Robert Kissin, an English businessman, who assisted me in the publication of my book in Great Britain, and Peter Conradi, an English writer who agreed to translate and prepare my book for publishing.

This book is not just my memoirs, it is a guide to introduce readers to my country, past and present. It is addressed to foreign readers and some of the events described should be of interest to them. I hope that my country will not be a *terra incognita* for them. My compatriots could also learn interesting facts about their history.

As I mentioned before, this book was written by chance, but that does not mean that it is not my favourite 'child'. This book is very important to me – and it is my hope that my readers will share my feelings.

NURSULTAN NAZARBAYEV

PART ONE

TOWARDS INDEPENDENCE

CHAPTER ONE

EARLY LIFE

CLOSE to Almaty, the Kazakh capital, lie the peaks of Ala Tau. It was here that I was born, in a mountain camp, in 1940. However, my earliest memory is not of the incredible beauty of the mountains, but of something else altogether – hunger.

As a child in those hard, post-war years, I used to wake before sunrise, harness the donkey and go to the nearby town. By the time the bread stand opened at 6 a.m., I would be there. The line was huge. If I was lucky, I would finally get bread by noon. It was heavy black bread which dented when you squeezed it. I would queue up two or three times so I could bring home ten loaves. The bread could not be stored for long so it was sliced into small pieces and dried in the sun. Eating such a bread gave us great pleasure, but the excitement was even greater when our cow had calves. From the milk we made *ayran*, a sour Kazakh drink, which we would mix with corn husks, *talkan*. If it had not been for this drink, then we would all have perished – not just my family, but all the families who lived like us.

It is considered shameful for a Kazakh not to know seven generations of ancestors. Even today, in a modern family, it is not unusual to find an old grandmother, an *apai*, who can tell the small children about their grandfather, great-grandfather and even great-great-grandfather. And so it was with me.

My ancestors lived at the foot of the Ala Tau range, in the village of Chemolgan, in the Kaskelen district of the Almaty region. All the members of my clan were mountain people, which made us an exception in Kazakhstan where most people are from the steppes. Our family rarely came down from the mountain pastures and quite frequently they spent their winters in the canyons.

Traditionally, a child's surname was derived from his father's name. If we had not changed our names in accordance with the traditional Russian style of first name, patronymic and surname, adopted throughout the Soviet Union, then my last name would not have been Nazarbayev, but Abishev.

The vast plains which form modern-day Kazakhstan have been home to nomadic peoples for more than 2,000 years. The Saksky tribes, who settled in the eighth to third centuries BC, were the ancestors of many of the different peoples of today's Kazakhstan and Central Asia. Fierce warriors, they were organised in a tribal hierarchy under a supreme commander. As far as we can tell, they worshipped many gods, including the sky.

It was around the tenth and eleventh century that Islam arrived in the territory of modern-day Kazakhstan, spreading from the Arab desert through to Central Asia, creating world-famous centres of Islamic culture such as Samarkand and Bukhara. The city of Turkestan was within Kazakhstan itself. Islam greatly influenced Kazakh culture, and was most evident in rituals linked to the burial of the dead and the birth of children, as well as other traditional ceremonies. Despite the determined efforts to stamp out religion during the Soviet years, many Kazakhs continued as practising Muslims.

However, the Kazakhs cannot be considered orthodox Muslims in the same way as Arab peoples. Even after the arrival of Islam, the traditional beliefs of sun worship and shamanism continued to exist alongside it. In effect, Islam was adapted to our own traditional way of life and, to this day, continues to retain some elements of our ancient beliefs – for example, for many Kazakhs it is forbidden to spit in wells or on the fire; indeed, a person is believed to be purified by jumping across fire. I remember, when I was a child, that my mother used to forbid me to point my hands towards the stars because she believed that they were holy.

The road to moral rejuvenation lies in resurrecting a sense of healthy pride in one's own nationality and traditions. Although much damage was done during the Soviet years, it is not too late to repair it.

Nowadays, people are returning to religion and not only to Islam which, in itself, is a very positive thing. The religious revival is absolutely necessary for the people of Kazakhstan, especially the younger generation. Religion also plays an important part in education.

Many in the West who do not know Kazakhstan sometimes express concern about the growth of Islamic fundamentalism across the whole of former Soviet Central Asia following the collapse of the Soviet Union. However, their fear is misplaced. There is no doubt that the influence of Islam is growing in Kazakhstan, but we must distinguish between religion, which is a positive thing, and fundamentalism, which poses a great danger to the country. Anyone who has any doubts about the latter need only look at Tajikistan, where religion has played a major role in fuelling years of virtually permanent civil war which have reduced large parts of the country to ruin. The recent crises in Chechnya and in the former Yugoslavia had similar beginnings.

By the thirteenth century, the region was incorporated into the Mongol empire of Genghis Khan. The Kazakhs, who were initially a mixture of Mongol and Turkic peoples, emerged in the 1400s. Then, in the following century, the first Russian incursions began, with the Cossacks leading the advance.

The Cossacks first settled in the western part of the country along the Ural River. By the end of the seventeenth century, they were formally protecting the Russian frontier in return for title to land and for land itself. One hundred years later, a line of Cossack settlements and fortifications was established across the northern boundary of the steppe region in order to defend the Russian border. Among the advance posts set up were those at Omsk, Zhelezinsk, Iamyshevsk and Semipalatinsk.

At the same time, the Dzungar invaders were pouring in from the East. The precise nature of events which followed have been the subject of dispute and also of falsification by Communist-era historians. According to the official Soviet version, some of the Kazakh hordes tried to seek the protection of the Russian empire against the Dzungars. First to sign was Abulkhayr Khan, leader of the Little Horde. Under the agreement, made in 1731, the Kazakh Khan promised to protect the Kazakh-Russian borders, defend trade caravans in the plains, provide troops when needed and pay tribute in animal skins. In return, Russia confirmed a perpetual line of Khans in his tribe and built a fort at the confluence of the Or and Yaik (Ural) Rivers for his defence. Other sultans followed his example over the next few years.

It is obvious why such a version of history appealed to Soviet historians, who were determined to create a Kazakh debt of gratitude running back for many centuries. Research by Kazakh historians has proved that the reality was far more complex. One theory, recently put forward, is that there was a secret pact between the Russians and the Chinese to provoke the Dzungars and the Kazakhs into fighting one another. At times the Russians helped the Kazakhs, and at other times they helped the Dzungars.

In any case, the tide began to turn in the Kazakhs' favour from 1726–30, with their first victories over the Dzungars. By 1757, the Dzungar Khanate had collapsed completely and the Dzungar people were exterminated by the Chinese. The main reason for their collapse was the Dzungars' error, repeated by Hitlerite Germany almost two centuries later, of waging war simultaneously on two fronts. The Dzungars simply could not cope with both the Kazakh insurrection against them and the strength of the Chinese forces.

A major role was played by Ablay Khan, the most prominent of the Kazakh leaders. Not only was he an effective military commander, he was also a cunning diplomat. Ablay weakened the Dzungars by playing on the rivalries and competition between the Dzungar princes. Then, as their empire crumbled, he began to prop it up, offering protection to those Dzungar princes who arrived in the Kazakh states on the grounds that it was better for Kazakhstan to have a weak Dzungar buffer state protecting it from China rather than a direct land border.

Although Ablay died in 1781, there were 80 more years of Khanate power. It was in many ways a golden period with a political system which contained some democratic elements. Many tales and legends from the period have been passed down from generation to generation by the great singers of the steppes.

However, Russia was getting stronger. From the early years of the nineteenth century, Russian forces mounted a large-scale offensive southward, building more forts as they went: Petropavlovsk, Ust-Kamenogorsk, Akmola and others in the north, were followed by Karkaralinsk in central Kazakhstan and then Karaganda. In 1853, they had reached the south of today's Kazakhstan, building the Perovsk fortress, which grew into today's city of Kzyl-Orda. Another fortress, Vernyi, meaning 'faithful', was built on the site of what has since become Almaty, which was for many years, until recently, the Kazakh capital. They prepared the area around these fortresses for the settlement of farmers. From 1867–68, all of present-day Kazakhstan was effectively under Tsarist Russian control.

What began as Cossack outposts quickly grew into peasant settlements as Russians, Ukrainians and other Slavic immigrants came to the steppes in increasingly large numbers. The newcomers were not only paid substantial subsidies to occupy the lands, but were also given the best and most fertile plots, while much of the local population was pushed into semi-desert regions.

The Kazakhs did not passively accept their fate at the hands of the Russians; indeed, the nineteenth century was marked by a series of insurrections. The Kazakhs' most effective leader was Sultan Kenisari Quasim-Uli, a grandson of Ablay Khan and one-time friend of the Russians. He fought the Russians across wide stretches of the plains from around 1836 until 1846. A highly effective military leader, he focused the Kazakh resistance, building on widespread discontent among the Kazakhs at the pillaging and slaughter which accompanied Russian rule. However, compared to the Russians, the Kazakhs were badly equipped and poorly armed. There were also frequent disagreements between the clans. Despite several victories, Kenisari was eventually forced to flee south, meeting his death at the hands of Kirghiz monks in 1847.

Although a few decades of relative quiet followed, resentment at Russian rule was building up, not just in Kazakhstan but also across Central Asia. It was exacerbated during the early years of the twentieth century by the acceleration of the influx of Slavic newcomers with their land and privileges. By the outbreak of World War I, the whole region was a powder-keg. It was ignited in June 1916 by a government decree ordering that the Central Asians, who were not liable to military service in the Tsarist army, be mobilised into labour battalions. The disturbances, which began in Uzbekistan, spread quickly through the region, provoking a brutal reaction from the Russians. The loss of life on both sides was enormous.

The most prominent of the Kazakh leaders was Amangeldi Iman-Uli, who started skirmishes with Russian detachments and captured the Kustanay and Turgay regions. The Russians eventually drove out his troops, but Amangeldi refused to lay down his arms until after the provisional government in 1917 declared a general amnesty. Ultimately, though, the Kazakhs proved the losers; some 300,000 Kazakhs were expelled from their ancestral lands, many of them leaving for the Xinjiang province of China.

The Soviet version of history stated that when the Bolshevik revolution – or rather *coup d'état* – broke out in November 1917 in Petrograd, the Kazakhs supported it and even sent troops. Reality was very different. The whole concept of revolution dawned on the Kazakh people much later when soldiers began returning from the front; most of them were Russians anyway or railway workers on the line which crossed the north-east of the republic.

The Kazakhs were largely indifferent to revolution. Although there were some elements of the Kazakh intelligentsia who supported Soviet power as a progressive force, other members of the intelligentsia, as well as the population as a whole, were instinctively suspicious of what was an alien and distant concept, the product of an alien culture with an alien language. They saw the Soviets as too powerful, belligerent and militarised – as it turned out, their suspicions were well-founded.

In the aftermath of the confusion brought by the Bolshevik revolution, a so-called autonomous Turkestan Republic was established in eastern Kazakhstan, but it was quickly absorbed by the Bolsheviks, who had no interest in granting sovereignty to national groups. In 1920, the area of present-day Kazakhstan was established as an autonomous republic, which was known until 1925 as the Kirgiz Autonomous Soviet Socialist Republic (ASSR). It was only in 1936 that Kazakhstan was admitted to the USSR as a full union republic, a status which it retained until the break-up of the Soviet Union at the end of 1991.

When Nazarbai, my grandfather, died suddenly, our family had to return to the valley and end its nomadic lifestyle. My father, Abish, was just three years old. When he was eleven he went to work for an affluent Russian family. The village of Chemolgan, where they lived, was already multi-ethnic. Kazakhs lived on one side of the Kaskelenka River; settlers from Central Russia, the Don and Ukraine lived on the other. They got on well together; there was enough land and water for everyone.

My father was lucky. The Nikiforovs, the family for whom he worked, were industrious and kind. He quickly learned to speak Russian and to take care of a peasant homestead. He eventually became indispensable to them: he knew how to make boots, plough the land, run a mill and come back with a profit when he went to trade at the market. He was also a great singer, with a wide repertoire of both Russian and Kazakh songs. When it was time for him to marry, he chose a bride named Alzhan. She, too, had lost her father, and was the best singer in the village. (I inherited some of my parents' musical talents and am not a bad *domra* player.)

They were far from idyllic years. People rarely had time to sing and dance. As my father said, they worked so hard that their calluses bled, but to work hard was considered honourable. The Nikiforovs had three sons of their own, but it was Abish who was always appointed the chief. My father never consciously suffered discrimination at the hands of the Russians and was paid fairly for his work. In fact, Russian and Kazakh families might have continued to live and work peacefully alongside one another, if it had not been for the fateful spring of 1929.

It was then that the people of Chemolgan first heard this strange, unpronounceable word 'collectivisation'. No-one had any idea what it meant. All this talk of 'transition from feudalism directly to Communism' meant nothing to them. They were soon to find out its true meaning. In the course of the next few years, a way of life which had evolved over centuries was destroyed almost without trace. Private farmers were made to give up their land and to live together in so-called collective farms. The process was motivated entirely by Communist ideology, rather than economic logic; the Soviet system was determined to eradicate private property. The suffering and destruction which it caused, however, was enormous.

The Nikiforovs were among the first to be uprooted by the over-zealous collective farm organisers. Cartloads of people left the village after losing everything that they owned. Some were sent to other parts of Kazakhstan, others even further to the north. As a poor labourer, my father was not persecuted. Instead, he was invited to join the Committee of Poor Farmers and asked to take over the mill which had been confiscated from his employer. However, he was not tempted by the idea of taking someone else's property.

New settlers arrived in Chemolgan. They were *kulaks* – the term the Bolsheviks applied to 'rich farmers' – from other areas, but they were not allowed to farm. They were instead forced to build a road in the mountain with picks and spades. Decades later, the locals still refer to this winding road as the 'convicts' highway'.

The ferocity of collectivisation was due in part to the specific nature of the Kazakh economy. By 1926, just under a quarter of the Kazakh population was engaged solely in agriculture, about 40 per cent depended on livestock alone and a third depended on livestock and agriculture. Although less than 10 per cent were wholly nomadic, some two-thirds were semi-nomadic, and migrated with their herds in the summer.

Bolshevik historians misunderstood the nature of traditional Kazakh nomad culture. They believed that the Kazakhs did nothing but move around the steppes at random, like gypsies. In reality, their life was far more structured. Most had a permanent winter home, with out-buildings, normally built out of wood, known in Kazakh as a *kystau*. They usually had a fixed summer habitat as well. Typically, the Kazakh nomad possessed large herds of cattle and so needed a vast territory on which to graze them. It was simply impossible for them to stay in one place. The system was also highly regulated. Everybody knew exactly to whom each piece of land belonged and where the border ended, making it impossible for members of one family or clan to cross into land belonging to another. Indeed, borders were always an extremely important matter. Disputes about them, *dzhirdau*, lay at the heart of some of the worst crises or conflicts on the steppes.

Tradition has always been important to Kazakhs. One of the most important traditions is the preservation of bonds between relatives. All the members of the family gather together to share in the joys and sorrows of each of their members. It is not only a question of teaching children to respect adults and to honour women. The oldest son takes full responsibility for the well-being of his younger brothers and sisters. The youngest son, too, has an important role: even after he has started his own family, he will stay in the home in which he was born. This home, the *shanrak*, in which the youngest son, father, mother and possibly even their parents live, remains the centre of the family.

The Bolsheviks were determined to get rid of this system. The main reason was undoubtedly ideological: they saw the nomadic agricultural system as little more than the relic of a bygone age which had to be swept away. Also, while the traditional hierarchical system was in place, it was difficult for them to impose their new methods of political control. There were also economic reasons. The Bolsheviks saw Kazakhstan as a vast potential food-producing reserve for the whole of Siberia and the Soviet Far East. By forcing the nomads to settle, they hoped to bring about a massive increase in grain production. The experts were not so convinced: many agronomists warned of the economic dangers of destroying the clan-based authority which controlled the livestock economy and pointed out that much of the ground which had been used for animal husbandry was not suitable for grain. There was also the problem of the resistance which the Kazakhs would inevitably put up to any attempt to break up their traditional society.

The leading Bolsheviks realised this. In 1923, just before his death, Lenin warned the more impatient members of the Communist Party leadership not to try to impose Russian-style 'class struggle' on the peoples of Kazakhstan and Central Asia. 'Can we approach these people and tell them that we shall overthrow their exploiters? We cannot do this,' he said in a speech to the Eighth Congress of the Russian Communist Party. 'In such cases we have to wait until the given nation develops.'

But with Lenin's death, any sense of moderation was forgotten. Under his successor, Stalin, it became Communist Party policy to 'eradicate the economic and cultural anachronisms of the nationalities'. Thus, at the November 1929 plenary session of the Communist Party's Central Committee it was formally decided to confiscate the nomadic lands of Kazakhstan and build a number of giant grain farms, which by 1932 were meant to supply 1.6 million tonnes of grain – an economic nonsense in a territory which was not suited to the production of grain. A 'plan' for settling the nomads was contained in the revised Five Year Plan and a special committee on settlement was set up in Almaty.

The plan was taken up enthusiastically by local Communists in Kazakhstan. One of their leaders was Fyodor Goloshchekin, who headed the Territory Communist Party Committee, between 1925 and 1933. His favourite saying was 'Better too much salt than too little.' According to Goloshchekin, the broom of the October Revolution should sweep up the Kazakh village – a principle which ended in great tragedy for the Kazakh people.

In December 1929, the Central Committee of the Kazakh Communist Party met to pledge the implementation of the plenum of the previous month. They added to the general line on collectivisation the proviso that the 'settlement' of the nomads was a necessary prerequisite. So, in January 1930, the Kazakh Central Executive Committee decided that out of 566,000 nomadic and semi-nomadic households, 544,000 should be settled by the end of the first Five Year Plan.

The process of settlement and collectivisation began. It was a chaotic and ill-thought out process carried out with scant regard for the objections of the people. The collectives which were created in the spring of 1930 lacked houses, sheds, agricultural implements and even arable land. Many were set up in desert and semi-desert locations without adequate water. Fodder was often not provided and driving herds to pasture was forbidden. Some even had no seed, livestock or any capital at all. The plan called for the construction of less than 2,000 residences and 70 barns; even so, only 15 per cent of the residences and 32 per cent of the barns were completed. For the 32,000 nomads settled in 1930–32, 2,500 houses were provided and just 108 baths. Organisation was poor, and there were few agronomists or agricultural experts. Most of the collective farms, *kolkhozes,* lacked a plan at all.

The resistance of the local people was fierce. Many of the Communist Party activists charged with carrying out the policy of collectivisation met with armed resistance and some of them were killed. From 1929 until 1931, about 80,000 people took part in 372 different uprisings in Kazakhstan. Roving bands of Kazakhs attacked *kolkhozes* and took away or killed the livestock.

The Soviet authorities hit back hard. They blamed the resistance on Alash Orda, a moderate political group, which had been founded in 1917 on the wave of a revival in Kazakh national consciousness. In reality, most of the group's members were drawn from the intelligentsia and were loyal to the Soviet regime. However, a scapegoat was needed to explain away the problems with collectivisation and Alash Orda fitted the bill. It was duly denounced as a 'centre of counter-revolution in Kazakhstan'. In 1930, the authorities announced that they had detected a 'plot' involving major nationalist figures who had organised resistance in the migrating villages, the *auls.* Inevitably, too, the local officials were blamed; more than 100 of them were arrested in two provinces alone. By the end of 1932 many of the republic's leaders had also been 'purged'.

The Kazakhs reacted in their own way. Rather than hand over their livestock to the new collective farms, many simply slaughtered them; in many areas, as many as 50 per cent of the animals were killed during the first few weeks of collectivisation. Many more animals failed to survive the winter because of poor organisation.

Nor was the Communist Party winning many ideological converts among the Kazakhs. In January 1929 there were only 16,550 Kazakh Communists. By 1931, this had only risen to 17,500, both Russians and Kazakhs, in the whole of rural Kazakhstan, only a quarter of them in predominantly Kazakh areas.

Official policy swung violently during the year. Nomads were first forced into strict, 'artel-type' collective farms, but at the 16th Party Congress in June/July 1930 it was belatedly decided to allow a more liberal form, known as 'TOZ', in the semi-nomadic areas. In June the local leadership decided to return farm implements and livestock to private hands in the nomadic and semi-nomadic areas. But in November 1930 they recollectivised the implements and, the following June, the livestock, too. By April 1930, 50.5 per cent of the rural population had been forced into collective farms. The numbers dipped to just over 29 per cent by August that year, but had reached 65 per cent by 1 October, 1931.

The rules were relaxed in the mid-1930s, allowing Kazakhs to take back some of their livestock. When the new collectivisation drive began in 1931, many tried to get around the rules by putting their animals out to pasture in distant ravines and woods. But they had to slaughter them when the winter came, living off the frozen meat until spring. As shortages of livestock, seed, implements and construction materials grew, people were simply shifted from one collective farm to another in the hope – usually in vain – that more grain or livestock would be made available. The suffering was both accompanied and accentuated by a dramatic drop in the number of cattle, the animal at the heart of the Kazakh agricultural economy. In 1928, there were 6,509,000 of them recorded in Kazakhstan. By 1932, the figure had dropped to only 965,000. The number of sheep fell in the same years from 18,500,000 to 1,386,000.

By the spring of 1932, the full extent of the damage became clear. Some 87 per cent of all *kolkhozes* and 51.5 per cent of non-collectivised, largely-nomadic households, were without livestock. The area under cultivation had increased by only 15–17 per cent, providing scant compensation. The republic was plunged into a massive, man-made disaster.

Even the official Soviet statistics from the time cannot hide the extent of suffering, which exceeded that of the other republics, including those in former Soviet Central Asia. The 1926 census showed 3,963,000 Kazakhs in the Soviet Union, the 1939 one just 3,100,000 – and that figure was certainly inflated. The real loss appears to have been much greater, with the number of Kazakh households falling from 1,233,000 in 1929 to 565,000 in 1936.

Robert Conquest, the British historian and chronicler of Stalin's terror, has estimated that, allowing for natural growth, the estimated 'population deficit' as a result of famine and purges was about one and a half million out of a population which, by 1930, was just over four million. Actual deaths, omitting the unborn and those who escaped to China, Mongolia, Turkey, Iran, some republics of Central Asia and the Russian region – Povolzhye, Siberia, and the Urals – must have been at least one million.

The whole of the Soviet Union was beset by terrible times as a result of Stalin's experiment, but Kazakhstan was one of the worst-hit regions, as the Bolsheviks rode roughshod over the traditions of the people in their quest for ideological conformity. Communities were destroyed and Kazakh culture and the Kazakh way of life were decimated. It took the Kazakh people decades to recover from the blow which was dealt to them during those few short years.

At the 17th Party Conference in February 1934, the troubles of Kazakh collectivisation were blamed largely on failure to settle the nomads. The next year, 1935, the concession allowing the creation of the more liberal 'TOZ' farms was withdrawn and they were converted into the usual 'artel-style' collectivised farms. By 1938, collectivisation was complete, but at what cost?

At that time, my father took his family into the mountains and took up livestock herding and a nomadic lifestyle. These events marked him for the rest of his life.

CHAPTER TWO

THE MEN OF STEEL

M Y CHILDHOOD was a harsh one. Shortly after I was born, a disaster struck the family: the winter camp where we used to tend the animals for the collective farm caught fire. My father was burned badly trying to put it out; despite all the efforts of the doctors, he was no longer able to bend his arm and it began to wither. This was the reason he was not drafted into the army when the Soviet Union entered the war the following year, in 1941.

But that did not mean he and my family were spared suffering. Years later, my parents described to me how those years had been like long winter nights, marked by hunger and cold. Their worst fear was of the wolves: my mother used to turn pale every time she heard their howls. She was not afraid of the wolves themselves, because she realised that my father, even with only one good arm, could kill them. She was worried instead that they would kill a sheep. And then what would we say to the collective farm bosses? No excuses were accepted. Any shepherd who did not protect his flock faced ten years in a forced labour camp.

Only the brief mountain summer brought some joy. The summers were not only beautiful, they also brought good food. In those days, sugar, bread and tea were delicacies which we could only dream of. What we did have in abundance were sweet roots, juicy berries and other treats which my mother taught me to gather. What I treasure most from my childhood were the blue summer skies over the snow-capped Ala Tau mountains, the bright sunshine and the wonderful fresh mountain air.

I was already five when I left the mountains for the first time. It was Victory Day and we went to the village of Chemolgan. I had never seen so many people. The war, coupled with Stalin's policy of mass-deportations, had brought many different groups of people there, whether Chechens, Germans, Balkans or Meskhetian Turks. There had also been a relaxation of the regulations after the war, so some of the *kulaks* who had been exiled during the 1930s were able to return to Chemolgan. The Nikiforovs were among those who returned – with the exception of the father, who had died far from home.

Half a century later, the Soviet Union was swept by a series of ethnic conflicts; language became a deeply political issue. Back in my childhood, it was very different. People were used to speaking different languages with one another. My father, for example, spoke a little of the language of the Balkars, who had been deported, and was accepted by them. Within a year of arriving in Chemolgan, I was speaking Russian with the other children, as well as snatches of Chechen and German.

After the war, during the late 40s and early 50s, my mother was given a hectare of beets to work for the collective farm. It meant back-breaking work from spring until the first snowfall. After sowing, she had to work the whole hectare of beets by hand, under the scorching sun, without once straightening. her back. The memory of experiences like that lasts a life-time. When the beets ripened, they had to be cut with a big knife, loaded up and handed over to the collective farm. In return, all we received was a certificate for one and a half sacks of sugar from the Burundai sugar mill.

My father worked hard too. Most of his time was spent with the livestock. He was also supposed to plant several hectares of wheat on a mountain slope and hand over the entire yield to the farm. When the wheat ripened, my father and I cut it by hand, all through the night by moonlight. While we worked, my mother would make sheaves which we took to the collective farm where they were put into the threshers. He still found the time to grow apples as well; even though he was almost illiterate, he knew how to cross fruit trees and used to take the apples by cart to the market, 45 kilometres away in Almaty.

We worked hard on the collective farm, but it was only thanks to our small family plot that we managed to survive. It was only half a hectare in size, but, little by little, we began to lose it. We also had to give up the horse which my father loved so much because we were not allowed to keep an animal; the farm needed the fodder. One day, I could not believe my eyes when I saw my father cutting down his own apple trees. He did this so that he would not have to pay taxes on them. By then, we had hardly anything to eat at all in the house, just tea and sometimes sugar. We had to give so much butter from our cow to the collective farm that all we had left was skimmed milk.

I remember later, when I was a young steel worker and went as a delegate to the Congress of the Young Communist League in Moscow, I came home with many stories to tell. I became very excited telling my father and our guests all about Khrushchev, about his speeches to the Congress and, in particular, his optimistic predictions about agriculture and closing the gap between town and country. I was so overwhelmed by the attention that I was getting from my elders that I did not notice the mockery in their eyes. My father had been watching me with barely concealed contempt. Then, when I started criticising the idea of allowing people to have their own private farm plots, Abish could not contain himself any longer.

'That's enough, son,' he said. 'We hear too many of those speeches on the radio. You tell us this: has everyone in Moscow lost their memory? Do they want the people to starve to death again like they did in the 1930s? A farmer without a plot is like a shepherd without any sheep. Don't take this personally, Sultan (that was what they used to call me), but this is not good news that you have brought back with you.'

I made up for this mistake many years later when I finally brought back some good news from Moscow. I had met Mikhail Gorbachev, who was at the time in charge of

Soviet agriculture, in the Kremlin where we talked about boosting meat output in Kazakhstan. I suggested what was really a seditious idea: we should not limit the private plots of farmers but, on the contrary, do everything to encourage them. If a villager wanted to have two cows, then that should be fine; if he wanted ten, then even better. This was long before the plenary session of the Communist Party Central Committee which gave the green light to the private sector, but Gorbachev was, nevertheless, ready to support me.

As soon as I got back from Moscow I went to see my fellow villagers, who had elected me as their representative to the national parliament, and told them about this resolution. When I saw their happy faces, I acutely missed my father, who was no longer alive. Sadly, the wise Abish never lived to see this day and to hear the news that was so reassuring to farmers.

Many things are difficult to explain in life. Even today, it is difficult for me to understand the logic of a system which meant that industrious people like my parents could end up with so little.

School was not hard for me. When I started school, my parents did not yet have their own home. They were nomads who spent the summer in the mountains and the winter in the steppes, so I lived with my paternal uncle until I was in the fourth grade. He lived some way from the school, and I was awakened for school early in the morning by the roosters – there were no alarm clocks. Then I walked, half in my sleep, through the snow for six or seven kilometres. I would arrive at the school at about 5 or 6 a.m. If the guard was kind then he would let me into the school while he got the stove going. I could snatch some more sleep by lying next to it.

The only time left to do homework was at night because the tasks on the farm had to be finished first. I had to feed the cattle, clean the shed, fetch water and work in the garden. I learned to value time. I managed to get my homework done and even had an hour or so for reading. In those days, there was a huge difference between life in the cities and life in the countryside. Things that were accessible for boys in the city were often little more than a dream for us. We were much closer to the prose of everyday existence and the concerns of just putting some food on the tables which is why we had such modest demands for our future and had to be more realistic about evaluating our potential.

Although my mother and father could barely read, they had a great respect for people who were educated. My teachers were also insistent that I had the potential to go on to further studies. When I finished the compulsory seven-year education, the family was unanimous that I should continue studying. I had to go to Kaskelen, the nearest town, where there was a boarding school. It was not very far away, but it was the first time that I had lived away from my family.

When I finished school, all attention in Kazakhstan was focused on a new city, Temirtau, where one of the Soviet Union's biggest steel plants was under construction.

I saw an advertisement in a newspaper for the Temirtau Technical School which was accepting Young Communist League members to be trained for the plant. The course was for one year and all expenses were to be paid by the government. When I showed it to my father, he thought about it, then he sighed and said: 'Well, son, go ahead and see the world. If you have troubles, come back: this is your home.' Within a few days, I had gathered together the necessary papers and left.

Although I had my father's blessing to go to Temirtau, my parents were not enthusiastic about the idea. Karaganda, and the surrounding area, including Temirtau, had a bad reputation because there was a well-known *Gulag*, a prison camp, there. There was also a local criminal gang which instilled terror among the residents.

My first impression of Temirtau was of a tiny town in the middle of an enormous construction site. There were cranes, trenches, foundations, pits, heaps of metal, sand, mounds of construction waste and tents – but no roads. When I arrived, the first blast furnace and electric power plants were being built.

We had just started to work when all of us with a secondary education were offered the chance to go for training at the steel plant in Dneprodzerzhinsk, in Ukraine. The Kazakh leadership, wanting to have enough trained local people for the Temirtau plant, had decided to send us to the Soviet Union's major steel centres to learn 'on the job' about the steel industry. Four hundred of us were sent off: some to the Urals, the rest of us to Ukraine.

The Dneprodzerzhinsk plant made a bad impression on many of the newcomers, including myself. Few of us had been raised in a city and we had only a vague idea about the conditions in which Soviet industrial workers had to live and work. It is understandable how a young man from the steppes reacts on seeing a steel plant for the first time. The noise is thunderous, sparks are everywhere, and all sorts of things fly through the air and threaten to fall on you. Molten cast iron runs like water in a canal and it is terrifying to go near it. The prospect of spending my whole life in that environment was depressing.

During the time we spent there, we used to scan the newspapers for reports on how work was proceeding at the plant in Temirtau. Would we finish our training in time to be the ones who started up the plant? Would we be capable of running such a large enterprise? I was recently looking through some old newspaper files and recalled the tense, and at the same time festive, atmosphere of those days. Journalists did not spare their superlatives in describing the heroic builders of the country's huge new steel plant. Just reading their reports made us feel enthusiastic and proud to be involved in this major national effort.

Suddenly, in August 1959, rumours began circulating around the factory of trouble in Temirtau. We heard that troops had been sent to the city, that there were casualties and that construction had been stopped. In those days of rigid state control of the media, the fact that the newspapers had nothing to say about the plant seemed to confirm the truth of the rumours, which became more detailed by the day. Then, one of the workers, who owned a radio, described how he had tuned in to Voice of America and heard President Eisenhower asking Khrushchev, who was touring the United States at the time, about the reports of trouble. Although Khrushchev denied that anything had happened, we were now convinced.

Later, we found out what had happened. The young people who had gone to work in Temirtau had been becoming more and more unhappy with the living conditions there. Typically, for the Soviet system, the factory was being raised at lightning speed, while the workers themselves had to live in tents and hastily erected barracks. Often there were not enough protective outer garments to go around, supplies of food were terrible and the water was often contaminated. By the summer of 1959, many of the workers had simply had enough. So, on 29 July, a crowd of thousands of bricklayers, concrete layers and assemblers gathered on a square by the headquarters of the construction site to complain to the management. When they saw that no one was going to come out to talk to them, they took justice into their own hands, and started looting the grocery stores and consumer good shops. That night troops entered the city and shooting began. Even today, no one can say how many people were killed, although there were certainly tens of them. There were also some foreigners present: a group of Bulgarians who had been sent there by their country's Young Communist League. A curfew was declared and some people were arrested. Later, the 'ringleaders' were tried and punished. This, it should be remembered, was the period of the so-called Khrushchev 'thaw', a time when the then Soviet leader promised to build Communism on our planet within 20 years.

By the time we returned to Temirtau, life had largely returned to normal. To our surprise the shops were especially well-stocked: the food stores had black and red caviar, sturgeon and good quality cognac and wine; the clothes shops were full of imported items – a rare luxury in those days. The reason was clear. After the unrest had been quelled, the authorities took urgent measures to 'pay off' the workers in order to prevent the same thing happening again. Such was the importance of the plant that even Leonid Brezhnev, the future Soviet leader, had gone on an emergency visit to Temirtau to see what had gone wrong.

On 2 July, 1960, the blast furnace finally went into operation. It was the only one of its kind in Kazakhstan or Central Asia. The day was marked by big parades, rallies and speeches, but the festivities were soon over, and the average life of the workers remained miserable. Our own living conditions were particularly intolerable: after a short time in damp and dirty basement accommodation, we were moved to an unheated dormitory where we kept warm by sleeping in twos on iron cots covered with mattresses. There was no place even to hang out our clothes to dry. We left our canvas work-clothes out in the frost because it was easier to put them on when they were frozen than when they were wet and heavy. There were no recreational facilities – the only entertainment that people had was big fights. Murders and other serious crimes were rife.

We survived because we were young and strong, yet there is no justifying the hardships that we all suffered. Such a justification might have existed in the 1930s, when the Soviet Union knew that its very survival depended on industrialisation, but this was now the late 1950s and 60s, and still the Soviet system remained indifferent to the people in whose name it was supposedly ruling. The country confused the means with the end and turned people into an extension of an all-devouring economic machine which demanded more and more of human beings while giving less and less in return. It was a mistake that we must never repeat again.

Within six months of working in the blast furnace I was earning 450 roubles a month – an unbelievable sum for a 20 year old in those days. I used to send 200 roubles to my father. I earned every rouble – it was incredibly heavy and dangerous work. The temperature in the furnace was about 2000° Celsius and the chamber was filled with gas and dust. There was no time to complain or take a break. During a shift we had to drink half a bucket of water to compensate for all the sweat. After work, we needed half an hour in a cold shower to recover. In the summer in Kazakhstan, it is also hot outside, as high as 35° Celsius. The workers were permanently exhausted by the heat: their muscles never had a chance to relax, and some had constant nose bleeds. A few could not handle the strain, so they went home.

I remember my father coming to visit to see what my job was like. He came with me on the night shift. As fate would have it, we had a big accident and I was involved in the clean-up. He watched the whole ordeal and the next morning tried to persuade me to leave. 'Why are you torturing yourself?' he asked. 'I was an orphan at the age of three and have seen a lot in my life, but I have never experienced such hell. Give it up.'

In fact, my move out of the blast furnace came far sooner than I expected – although it was not something I initially wanted. I had joined the Communist Party in 1962 and became active in community affairs. I was a delegate to Congresses of the Young Communist League and was elected head of the Party organisation of my workshop and as a member of the Central Committee of the Young Communist League. Even today, I make no apologies for joining the Party. Some of the best workers there were Communists and I wanted to follow their example.

I certainly did not plan a political career; I was still working full-time as a steel worker. Nevertheless, all these outside activities were getting me noticed. One day I was summoned by the head of the city's Communist Party Committee and offered the post of first secretary of the city's Young Communist League. Becoming a full-time Party worker did not appeal to me. To be honest, it was partly because it would have meant a dramatic drop in my salary, but I also did not want to leave the steelworks and my colleagues.

At first I resisted, earning a serious reprimand for my disobedience. The Communist

Party was like an army in those days. It was simply not done to disagree even slightly with your superiors. We were all meant to be 'soldiers of the Party' and soldiers had to obey orders. In the end, I gave in, although only after receiving assurances that I would still be dealing with the plant and would not be leaving the steel industry.

And so I gradually began the move into public life, taking various jobs as I moved up the hierarchy. Along the way I acquired a college education at the Karaganda Polytechnic Institute, thanks to sponsorship by the plant.

In 1972 I became secretary of the Communist Party Committee of the Karaganda Metallurgical Kombinat and four years later I became Second Secretary of the Karaganda Regional Party Committee.

The most memorable event of those days was meeting Sarah, my future wife. This happened right by the blast furnace after an accident. Whenever there was an accident and metal spilled on the ground, the workers could not leave until they had cleaned up all the scrap metal and restarted the railway. This was a strict rule, no matter what time of day or night. If you made a mess, then you had to clean it up yourself. I had been on my feet for nearly 24 hours, was covered with soot, with only my eyes and teeth shining when I met this young woman. She had been on duty that night at the electrical sub-station and came over to see what the problem was. Not long afterwards, we had a big wedding. Since I was an outstanding worker and activist, it was sponsored by the Young Communist League. As was customary in those days, we were also presented with the keys to our own apartment.

However, when we went to the address which they had given us, we saw that construction work had barely begun on the five-storey building and its 80 apartments. After the wedding, we had to live with a friend who had a tiny one-bedroom apartment. He lived there with his wife, two children and their grandmother. We spent our wedding night in the same room as grandma. Despite that inauspicious start, my wife and I have been together for more than three decades. We have three daughters, and now grandchildren too. In 1972, I became the Communist Party leader of Kazakhstan's Magnitka.

In those early days, very little of my time was spent in an office shuffling papers. Instead, I spent day and night at the plant's various construction sites. Such was the all-embracing nature of the Communist Party's work that I was often not sure whether I was working with the manager or instead of him. The pace was dizzying: I could be at the blast furnace after an accident, at the converter, writing schedules late into the night, submitting hundreds of different legal documents, organising weekend overtime or overseeing the transport of concrete, metal and equipment. Every day I met dozens or even hundreds of people. They came to construction headquarters with diverse and sometimes unexpected problems and requests – a foreman might be threatening to take a crew off the job because the supply of concrete was not regular or a worker's wife might want us to persuade her alcoholic husband to stop drinking.

Such was the importance of the plant that not a month went by without a visit from at least one senior official from one of the Moscow ministries. The worst times were when we were up against a deadline before a big holiday, such as May Day, 7 November (the anniversary of the Bolshevik revolution), or the opening of a Communist Party Congress. Thousands of people were taken off less urgent tasks to finish a project on time. I remember having to complete one of our chemical plants, whatever the cost, so that one of the officials could report its completion to a Congress. He was able to make his report on time, but on the first day of the Congress one of the galleries collapsed.

In many respects, the plant was a microcosm of the problems of Soviet industry as a whole. During these rushed jobs something was always overlooked which would prevent us from producing the kind of steel which was required. The workers were under considerable stress; because there were so many accidents, they never had any weekends off and their wages were allowed to fall catastrophically. As a result, absenteeism was high, workers were continually late and staff turnover reached 30 per cent. The management, meanwhile, was forever being reshuffled in the hope that it would improve performance. We finally obtained results, not least by making dramatic improvements in the living conditions of the workers, but it only happened after a long struggle. However hard we worked, we could not change a whole economic system.

I discovered how typical the plant's problems were in 1976 after I was promoted to the Karaganda Regional Party Committee, with responsibility for the region's industry as a whole. Besides the steel plant, the region also had coal mines as well as other industry. The miners had a particularly bad time, as I found after six months which I spent visiting all 26 of the underground pits. The mines were in constant danger of explosions and collapses and the methane level was extremely high. The miners were forever being chided for not reaching the plan targets. When I looked into the matter, I realised that the problems in the coal basin were exactly the same as at the steel plant – the centralised allocation of capital investment and the distribution of funds. The slogan of 'less spending and more output' prevented new underground mines from being developed and the city began, literally, to be undermined. The ground sank, water pipes broke and roads and buildings collapsed. The miners' living conditions were appalling. We managed to make some improvement, as we had done at the steel plant, by appealing directly to Moscow, but the conditions still remained bad.

Looking back, it is clear that it was in the 1970s that the process of economic decline of the Soviet Union began in earnest. It ended with the collapse not just of the Soviet Union itself but of the whole socialist system.

In 1979, I was promoted to membership of the secretariat of the Kazakh Communist Party. Some two decades after I first set foot in the Temirtau plant, I left the Karaganda region and moved to Almaty. Then in 1984, the year before Gorbachev came to power in Moscow, I was appointed Prime Minister of Kazakhstan.

CHAPTER THREE

THE POISONED LEGACY

IN THE WEST of Kazakhstan, on the border with Uzbekistan, lies the Aral Sea. The world's fourth largest lake, it once contained as many as one trillion cubic metres of water which yielded 800,000 tonnes of fish a year. Whole communities of people used to live around its shores. From the beginning of the 1960s, the sea began to die.

The long chain of events which led to the destruction of an entire sea was started by economic planners in faraway Moscow. In order to create vast cotton fields in the dry lands of Soviet Central Asia, they ordered the digging of long irrigation canals which were fed by the waters of the two main rivers, the Amu Darya and the Syr Darya, which flow into the Aral Sea. There were some scientists who warned about the consequences of such an action and about the inevitable effect on the environment, but their speeches were made behind closed doors. None of the political leaders wanted to hear them and so a resolution was passed by the Soviet Politburo to proceed with the irrigation projects.

From the point of view of the planners, it was an undoubted success. Production soared – not only of cotton but also of rice – in Uzbekistan, Tajikistan and Turkmenistan. The entire socialist camp lived off that cotton. Pressure was put on all the Central Asian republics, even mountainous Kyrgyzstan and Tajikistan, to produce more and more cotton so that we could supply Cuba, North Korea and Moscow's other allies as well. As a result, the Soviet Union became the world's second largest exporter of cotton, after China. But this was still not enough for the Kremlin. The goal was to push production in Uzbekistan up to six million tonnes and in Kazakhstan to one million. This meant making use of water which should have gone into the Aral Sea.

Before the irrigation projects began, the Aral Sea had been as big as North America's Lake Huron. From 1960 it began to shrink. Over 20 years, its level dropped by more than 16 metres, its area shrank by 45 per cent and its volume fell by 75 per cent. By 1989 the huge network of irrigation channels which had been built by the over-zealous Soviet engineers meant that the Aral Sea was only receiving 20 per cent of the amount of water each month that it had used to receive in 1960. By the 1990s, the Aral Sea had retreated as much as 150 kilometres (95 miles) from its old shores. If matters had continued at this rate, the sea would have dried up completely within 25 years. Over two decades, the salinity of the Aral Sea rose threefold to 25 grams a litre, killing the fish stocks.

The fishing industry, which once supported 60,000 people, has been decimated; some erstwhile fishing villages were left tens of kilometres from the shore. Their population dwindled as the people who had lived there drifted away in search of work. One of the most potent symbols of the shrinking of the Aral Sea are the abandoned fishing boats left high and dry. The only way to keep the processing industry working was to import fish from the Pacific coast of Russia, thousands of kilometres to the East.

Equally damaging were the chemicals. The increasing demands for cotton could only be met with the saturation use of pesticides, fertilisers, and herbicides. Each hectare of cotton grown required 260 kilograms of fertilisers and other chemicals. These found their way not just into the Syr Darya and Amu Darya rivers, but also into the underground water table from which the people drew their drinking water.

It is not only a local problem. Every year, millions of tonnes of toxic dust from the exposed sea bed are whipped up by the wind or evaporate into the atmosphere. They are carried hundreds of kilometres away as far as the Tian mountain chain and into the glaciers which are the source of drinking water for much of the rest of Kazakhstan.

For more than 20 years, scientists, both in Kazakhstan and elsewhere in the Soviet Union, watched the problem of the Aral Sea getting worse and worse. Countless articles and books were written, but while the Soviet system reigned supreme, nothing happened.

During the 1970s, the Soviet leadership finally took action. The government gave the appropriate all-Union ministries and agencies the task of working with officials from Kazakhstan and the other affected republics to study the problem and work out how it could best be tackled. The result was a dramatic plan, the central feature of which was a proposal to divert some of the water from the great rivers of Siberia into the Aral Sea basin. Such a plan would not only have restored the level of the Aral Sea to its previous height, but it would also have helped irrigate all the arid lands of Central Asia.

The proposal called for the construction of a canal running some 2,550 kilometres from the River Ob. In 1976, it was estimated to cost 18.4 billion roubles, a huge sum of money. Nevertheless, it would have provided water not just to the republics of Central Asia and Kazakhstan, but also to some of the driest parts of southern Russia as well.

By the mid-1980s, the project was already running into heavy criticism. The newly-formed ecological movements, which grew rapidly during the liberal political climate of the Gorbachev years, attacked the project. So, too, did a few specialists, who argued that diverting water from the rivers would have a serious, negative effect on the ecosystem, not just of the region, but of the planet. Such criticism was overdone: it was planned to divert only around two per cent of the water in the rivers, with minimal environmental consequences. In any case, the main problem was more an economic than an ecological one; neither the Central Asian republics nor Russia had the money for the project at that time.

As Prime Minister of Kazakhstan I was closely involved in the development of the project. I continued to support it even after it had lost favour in Moscow. On 23 June, 1990, I joined the leaders of the Central Asian republics in sending a declaration to the leadership of the Soviet Union. 'We consider it necessary,' we wrote, 'to return to the question of diverting to Central Asia and Kazakhstan part of the water from the Siberian rivers as one of the principal methods to save the Aral Sea and solve the problem of feeding the local population. In our opinion, this will determine to a great degree the future of a region which is home to more than 50 million people.' Today I would still put my signature to these words.

Our plea was to no avail. The collapse of the Soviet Union effectively removed that option. If there was not enough money to complete the projects in the 1980s, there was even less in 1990. With the possibility of 'new water' ruled out, the only way to restore the level of the Aral Sea is to halt all the irrigation projects along the rivers which feed into it. But even if we took such a drastic step, it would still take years before the water rose to its previous level.

However, according to scientists, another technical solution for the problem does exist; indeed, it could have been used long ago without even sacrificing cotton output. Much of the water used in agriculture is wasted through evaporation, or else because it drains out of unlined irrigation canals. At least half the 120 cubic kilometre flow of the two rivers could be saved by rebuilding the canals and introducing new irrigation systems. This would, at least, begin to stabilise the Aral Sea at its present level, although it would not restore it. To achieve that, it would be necessary to shift Central Asia away from its excessive dependence on cotton to other crops more suited to its arid climate.

The collapse of the Soviet Union at the end of 1991 changed the nature of the problem of the Aral Sea, turning it from a domestic, Soviet issue into an international one. It gave us the chance to tackle a problem which had been swept under the carpet for too long. However, it has not been easy. Our countries are all poor and have few resources. There is also the problem of how to translate international goodwill into concrete offers of aid.

However, we have taken the first step. After the collapse of the Soviet Union, and with it, the disappearance of the old Soviet structures, the ministries of Kazakhstan and the Central Asian States agreed to create an Inter-State Council to co-ordinate water use. This meant agreeing on how to share out the waters of the Amu Darya and the Syr Darya, taking into account the effect on the Aral Sea. But many more steps must follow.

In January 1993, I met the leaders of the four Central Asian States in the Uzbek capital, Tashkent, to discuss co-operation. Among the issues which we discussed, one of the most pressing was that of the Aral Sea, and we agreed then to create an International Fund to save it.

Our plan was formalised two months later when the five of us met in the city of Kyzl-Orda. As a sign of the Russian government's continued interest in the problem, the meeting was also attended by Georgiy Khizha, a Russian Deputy Prime Minister. We outlined joint efforts for tackling the problems of the Aral Sea and its basin in order to prevent the disaster from getting even worse, as well as taking measures to normalise the environment and ensure the socio-economic development of the most affected areas. We also adopted an appeal to the United Nations.

We continued to work on the issue. At our second annual meeting, in January 1994, in Nukus, capital of Uzbekistan's Karakalpak Republic, we set up a joint fund and permanent committee to try to save the sea and improve the health of people round it. At that meeting, we, together with Uzbekistan, Turkmenistan and Kyrgyzstan all pledged to allocate one per cent of our budgets to the fund, which was to be based in Kyzyl-Orda, and which I was to chair. Only war-torn Tajikistan was exempt. It was a significant step and one which showed our growing commitment to solving the problems of the Aral Sea.

Our decision to create an International Fund reflected our belief that the fate of the Aral Sea is not just a regional problem but a global one. The Aral Sea plays a major role in the preservation of the biosphere of the planet. Solving this problem requires the co-ordinated work of all mankind.

I had brought the problem onto the world stage myself when I mentioned it in a speech to the 47th session of the United Nations in October 1992. As Islam Karimov, the President of Uzbekistan, pointed out, it was only thanks to the collapse of the Soviet Union that we were eventually able to appeal for help to the world public. 'Could we have arranged a meeting of the five republics of Central Asia and Kazakhstan in Soviet times? Never. No one would have let it happen,' he told the meeting. 'In the conditions prevailing in the Soviet Union the problem was not even raised.'

Nevertheless, Russia itself is also concerned with the problem. Moscow's interest stems in part from a sense of moral responsibility for a neo-colonial system which was imposed on us during the Soviet years. The Russians also have sound material reasons for helping solve the problem of the Aral Sea: some 90 per cent of cotton grown in Central Asia and Kazakhstan is exported to the European part of the Commonwealth of Independent States.

Russian officials attended both the Kyzl-Orda and Nukus meetings, even though they did not make it to the third. All the problems relating to the Aral Sea are being co-ordinated with scientists and planning institutions in Russia. The government in Moscow has agreed to bear part of the expense of the project and has made clear that it, too, considers the problem as its own affair.

There has been no shortage of ideas and proposals from various international bodies to tackle the Aral Sea problem. Many individual governments, too, have offered to help: among them, the United States, Britain, Germany, France, Italy, Turkey, Den-

Fig. 1 Student days, Dneprodzerzhinsk, 1959.

FIG. 2 Temirtau, 1961.

FIG. 3 Karaganda's metallurgical plant. The Temirtau steel plant
where Nazarbayev first worked.

FIG. 4 The poisoned legacy – the Aral Sea. (PHOTO: *Still Pictures*)

Fɪɢ. 5 With Mikhail Gorbachev, working together for *perestroika*, during the
Congress of People's Deputies of USSR, Moscow, 1990.

FIG. 6 Meeting with Margaret Thatcher in Almaty,
September 1991.

FIG. 7 Taking the Constitutional oath at his inaugaration as President of Kazakhstan,
10 December 1991.

Fig. 8 First visit to Moscow, with President Boris Yeltsin,
March 1994.

mark, Israel, Belgium, Switzerland and the Netherlands. Specific projects are being funded by the World Bank and other international financial organisations. Even Israel has expressed a desire to join a Central Asian body co-ordinating Aral Sea projects. In June 1994, the World Bank organised a two-day summit in Paris aimed at saving the Aral Sea from totally drying up and pledged 32 million dollars towards that end.

Many people in the West have asked how they can be sure that the aid will find its way into the right hands, and want to know whether there will be controls on how the money is spent. To try and assuage such fears, the aid will go to integrated region-wide projects, chosen by the Inter-State Council and its executive committee, rather than being allocated individually to the five countries bordering the Aral Sea. So far seven projects have been chosen, including one dealing with water distribution and another aimed at ensuring that the water taken from the Amu Darya and the Syr Darya is used correctly and economically. We acknowledge that the donors themselves will be able to control how the money is spent far better than we could; for that reason, implementation of the projects will be funded and supervised by those who grant the money.

However, it is clear that foreign help alone will not be enough. The problem cannot be solved by a single international organisation, however large or powerful. It is up to all the states which border the Aral Sea to work together to solve it. Unfortunately, the will sometimes seems to have been lacking.

At the start of the 1995 summit, I surprised some of my partners with a speech in which I was highly critical of their failure to fulfil their financial pledges. Only 15 per cent of the expected amount of money had arrived in the account of the executive board of the International Save the Aral Sea Fund. The Republic of Kazakhstan donated 30 per cent, and Kyrgyzstan and Uzbekistan donated two per cent each. Turkmenistan and Tajikistan proposed using their 'entrance fees' within their own territory, which was not a particularly satisfactory solution.

Ultimately, we found a compromise: I agreed to accept the argument put forward by President Karimov that spending by individual states on environmental projects linked to the Aral, and not just those deposited in the fund itself, should still be counted as contributions.

Nevertheless, I feel I was right to speak out over the fact that we, the states which founded the fund, were not fulfilling our own financial obligations. Obviously, each of us could point to financial difficulties, but if we wanted to convince the rest of the world to help, then we had to show that we were playing our own part. By not paying ourselves, there was a danger that we were discouraging outsiders from doing so, as well.

Whatever our success in dealing with the water level of the Aral Sea, another equally important problem remains: the health of the people living in the sea's basin, which continues to deteriorate. According to some estimates, some 80 per cent of the women and children in the area suffer from anaemia. Infant mortality rates have soared and life expectancy has plunged.

The land around the Aral Sea is already so contaminated that the most rational solution would simply be to move all the people and abandon the area as a wasteland. Kazakhstan is a vast and sparsely populated country, and there is certainly no shortage of land for them elsewhere in the country. But we do not have the resources to build enough homes for all of them. And, even if we did, many people would simply refuse to go. The Kazakhs are very conscious of tradition. They want to die in the place where they were born.

Our first priority is to supply the local people with fresh drinking water. We also have to build hospitals, and provide adequate food, which they do not have. There is also a purely economic problem: if we are going to reduce the amount of water taken out of the rivers for irrigation, then we must find alternative work for those people, especially in Uzbekistan, who now work in the cotton industry. There is very little other employment in much of Uzbekistan, and the population of that republic is increasing dramatically. The Kazakhs who make their living from cultivating the rice which also uses this water face the same problem.

Underlying everything, though, is one central point: we must tackle the cause of the problem as well as the symptoms: and that means restoring the water level of the sea.

The shrinking of the Aral Sea, because of its scope, is one of the most serious ecological disasters being faced by our planet today. It is not an exaggeration to put it on the same level as the destruction of the Amazon Rain Forest. The factors which led to it were typical of the years when the Soviet Union was ruled by Leonid Brezhnev, an era which, during the Gorbachev years, became known as a period of stagnation.

The description was appropriate. Under the totalitarian administrative command system which Brezhnev created, it was not only the economy which stagnated, but also almost every other sphere of life. Even the people became apathetic. The situation worsened in the last few years before Brezhnev's death in 1982 when a fully fledged 'cult of personality' was created around the ageing and increasingly decrepit leader. This 'cult' was mainly shaped in Moscow by Brezhnev's team within the ruling Politburo and the secretaries of the Communist Party's Central Committee. But the disease spread throughout the whole Party and government structure, down to each of the 15 Soviet republics. Brezhnev selected the Central Committee leaders in the republics, and they, in turn, appointed the heads of the regional Communist Party committees entirely on the basis of personal loyalty.

This highly complex bureaucracy was devised in such a way as to ensure that all major decisions were taken from above. For example, in order to become first secretary of the regional Party committee, a candidate had first to be interviewed by the republic's Central Committee and then by the Soviet Communist Party Committee. As for the highest level appointments, candidates had to be interviewed by two or three members of the Politburo, then by the second-in-command and, finally, by the Party general secretary himself. After that the candidacy would be discussed at meetings of the secretariat and the Politburo. It had little in common with democracy. A recommendation from the national Central Committee made the appointment final, leaving the plenary session of the regional Communist Party committee with nothing more to do than wield its rubber stamp.

Sometimes the procedure was criticised locally, especially when some complete unknown was appointed from the outside. However, the concept of Party discipline required total submission to the higher bodies. Some parts of the country were completely beyond reproach because they were headed by close friends of the general secretary. This was true of Kazakhstan, Uzbekistan, Ukraine and several other regions.

In the later years, Brezhnev become more and more incapable. I remember a particular incident from 1980, when the entire Politburo travelled to Kazakhstan for celebrations marking the republic's 60th anniversary. Brezhnev made a terrible impression. He had no expression in his eyes and walked only with great difficulty, supported on both sides by two hefty men. As part of the celebration, a huge reception for one thousand guests was held in the foyer of the Auezov Theatre in Almaty. Everybody had just sat down when Dinmukhamed Kunayev, Kazakhstan's veteran Communist Party leader, proposed a toast to Brezhnev. No sooner had everyone taken a sip and put down their glasses, than the main guest of honour suddenly stood up and headed towards the exit. Naturally, everyone in the leadership followed him. Brezhnev went outside, got into his car, and a minute later, the whole cortège drove away. It was clear that he had simply forgotten where he was and why he had come. And this was the man who was meant to be running a nuclear superpower.

When Yuri Andropov succeeded Brezhnev at the end of 1982, he tried to implement major changes. But he could do nothing without changing the system of relations within the Communist Party apparatus and within society. Andropov had neither the time nor the energy. Already a sick man when he took over from Brezhnev, he died 15 months later. Konstantin Chernenko, his successor, lasted even less time. It is no wonder that Mikhail Gorbachev was greeted with such enthusiasm when he became general secretary in 1985. People began working better and it looked as if things would improve. The population as a whole seemed to trust the new Party leadership, and believed it was capable of bringing about a real improvement in the way in which the country was run. Unfortunately, it did not turn out that way.

Amid the anti-Communist euphoria which followed the defeat of the 1991 *coup*, many were deeply critical of those who had worked within the Communist Party apparatus during the years which immediately preceded the arrival of Gorbachev and the policy of *perestroika*, with which he aimed to transform the Communist system. However, there were undoubtedly honest people among them. One has to look at the circumstances in which these officials worked. Undoubtedly, they felt humiliated to see a great country like the Soviet Union being governed by leaders who were so old and sick that they could not say anything that they did not read from their notes. Nevertheless, the whole machine was so well-established that anyone who tried to oppose it was first reprimanded and then expelled from the Party, which meant the end of a career.

Many people, of course, took the easy way out and ignored everything that was going wrong in order to sit back and enjoy the privileges which they enjoyed as *apparatchiki* – members of the vast State and Communist Party *apparat*, or bureaucracy, which ran the country. Such people exist in every society, not just Soviet society. There is no disputing, though, that many decent people were misled, accepting unquestioningly the absurdities and injustices which developed over the decades of Soviet rule.

As I rose up through the Party and government structure in Kazakhstan, I came to understand more and more about the absurdities of the economic system. There was something completely arbitrary about the nature of many of the economic and industrial decisions.

For example, in 1980 after I became a secretary of the Central Committee of the Kazakh Communist Party, a veritable cascade of electrical power plants began to be built at the Ekibastuz hydro-electric power station. I remember asking about them during a meeting of the Party's Central Committee in Moscow. Why were so many plants being built but no repair system? I asked. Why were there not regular deliveries of equipment? Why was there no adequate housing for the workers, recreation facilities or childcare provisions? No one was able to give a real answer to any of my questions.

Often, in areas with surplus labour, we would erect huge plants employing 10–15,000 people instead of building small consumer plants, regardless of whether they were needed or not. For instance, it was decided to build a huge textile plant in the city of Kustanai, in the north of Kazakhstan, to give jobs to the women. But when they were sent there, it turned out that there were not enough jobs for the men. Shortly afterwards, I heard almost by accident that there were plans to build a diesel engine plant in Yelabuga, a few hundred kilometres away, across the border in Russia. This was precisely the kind of plant that we needed in Kustanai, so I went to Moscow to try and get the plans changed.

I went to see Andrei Kirilenko, who functioned *de facto* as Brezhnev's deputy for most of his time in office. He welcomed me into his office and, for some reason, even kissed me. I spent a long time telling him about our plans but I could see that he wasn't listening very attentively. At the end of this strange conversation, he suddenly asked me:

'So what is your problem?'

'I would like the diesel engine plant to be built in Kazakhstan,' I replied.

He immediately called Frolov, a department head from the Central Committee of the Communist Party, and Polyakov, the Minister of the Motor Industry. In just ten minutes the problem was resolved: the plant would be built in Kazakhstan. The resources involved were enormous and tens of thousands of peoples' lives were affected. This was how major economic decisions were taken in those days.

I was especially amazed after I became chairman of Kazakhstan's Council of Ministers – Prime Minister – in 1984. I had just started the job when the chairman of the republic's State Planning Committee came to me and requested bonuses for all of his assistants and department heads equivalent to their monthly salaries.

'What have they all done to earn these bonuses?' I asked in amazement.

'Don't you know that we are going to Moscow to defend the plan for next year?' he replied, almost indignantly.

'So what?'

'Well, we'll have to work with all the department heads at the State Planning Committee, invite them to our rooms and offer them hospitality.'

Two days later, the Finance Minister also came to my office:

'We're going to Moscow to defend the budget. Please give bonuses to me and my assistants.'

Such practices were essentially open policy. One year I happened to be in Moscow when the republics' plans were being defended at the State Planning Committee. On the first floor of the building there were generous helpings of food and traditional dances organised by whichever republic happened to be there that day. What was essentially bribery became such a problem that the bosses of the State Planning Committee forbade people to bring bags into the building. People reacted quickly to this restriction by simply leaving their present in the cloakroom and telephoning the person for whom it was intended, telling them to come down and pick it up. I will never forget how my predecessor told me in all seriousness how one national minister was fond of piglets and another liked to receive fresh tomatoes.

It is easy to see how such a supposedly 'scientific' approach to devising the plan and budgets could produce arbitrary results. It was especially hard for the chairman of our State Planning Committee and the Finance Minister to defend the Kazakh republic's plan and budget for 1985, because I refused to give them their bonuses.

Under the Soviet system, all the profits from enterprises, regions and republics, was sent to Moscow. Moscow then divided up the budget, funds and resources. If you were on good terms with the Finance Minister, you could get a few million extra roubles. If you were friends with the Chairman of the State Supplies Committee then you could have cement, metal and timber. No one particularly cared that they were taking someone else's share of the common pot; nor did they suffer any guilty conscience. Everyone was too busy trying to deal with their own problems.

The prevalence of this administrative-command system corrupted management. Whether you liked it or not, you had to follow the unwritten rules: you had to fawn on your superiors, give presents and offer hospitality, otherwise not you, but your republic, its industry and factories would be forced on to a starvation diet. The only way to get investment was to be clever and resourceful. This was the wellspring of degradation, crime and corruption. It was the system itself which forced so many people into crime.

As chairman of the republic's Council of Ministers, I saw how the USSR State Planning Committee and the USSR State Supplies Committee made it look, on paper, as if the all-important plan was being fulfilled, even when this was clearly not the case. Plans were approved despite the fact that everyone knew quite well that we only had seventy to eighty per cent of the necessary resources, making failure inevitable. Hence the imbalances throughout the country.

So corrupt was the system that even if the planned targets were not met locally, all was still not lost. People had contacts, so they would appeal to the Council of Ministers or to the State Committee on Statistics and to the Central Committee of the Communist Party in order to have the targets quietly revised and postponed. This was often at the expense of other enterprises.

The whole thing was worsened by the absurd way in which the economic indicators were calculated. Although officials would boast in their speeches about millions of tonnes, square metres or kilowatt hours of output of a product, performance was actually calculated in financial terms. In a Western-style market system this is logical, but in a planned economy, when prices are arbitrary and there is no competition, it makes no sense at all. The more a plant increased the cost of inputs needed to make each unit of production, the more it could charge and the more its turnover increased; in other words, the more inefficiently an enterprise worked, the better it seemed to be doing. Why make miniature switches for machinery when you could boost revenues hundreds of times by making enormous, outmoded ones instead? Why use inexpensive but sturdy materials for construction when you could hit your rouble-denominated targets much more easily by using huge concrete blocks and panels?

The whole Soviet system formed an enormous vicious circle. Every breakthrough cost us tremendous effort. It was increasingly clear that this vicious circle was caused by an absurd economic system which had developed a momentum of its own and almost completely turned its back on the real needs of the people whom it was supposed to be serving. Of all the 15 Soviet republics, Kazakhstan was the most vivid example of this.

The republic's wealth of resources provided the potential for the Soviet Union's mining, steel, energy, oil and chemical industries: during the first Five Year Plans of the 1930s, the vast reserves of copper in Dzhezkazgan stimulated the development of non-ferrous metallurgy. Resources from central and eastern Kazakhstan prompted the development of some of the Soviet Union's largest enterprises which supplied the country with around 30 per cent of its copper, 70 per cent of its zinc, over 60 per cent of its lead and 90 per cent of its titanium and magnesium. The deposits of phosphorous in southern Kazakhstan, especially in Karatau, provided the USSR with 90 per cent of its yellow phosphorous output; deposits in the Aktyubinsk region gave it almost all its chrome. There were also the coal basins of Karaganda and Ekibastuz and the huge oil and gas fields which began to be developed in the 1980s in western Kazakhstan. Kazakhstan was also of major importance to Soviet agriculture, with 10 million head of cattle, 40 million sheep and goats and some 40 million hectares of cultivated land.

There was no doubting Kazakhstan's economic might. However, few of these materials were actually processed within the republic. We were responsible for the extraction and enrichment of alumina, but it was processed elsewhere. We were just left with the huge environmental problems. The copper produced in the republic was also sent elsewhere in the Soviet Union in its raw form. Nor were we trusted with the production of gold and silver bars: again, we had to export the raw material to other republics, even though it would not have been difficult for us to process them.

At the same time, some 60 per cent of the consumer goods which were needed in Kazakhstan had to be imported from the other Soviet republics. They never sent us enough. All the republic's resources were ploughed into the giants of heavy industry while the people's genuine needs were put on hold. For decades, the huge factory buildings, the electrical power plants, the powerful blast furnaces and enormous cranes were portrayed by the Soviet propagandists as the source of our hope for a better future. But this hope faded bit by bit until it finally vanished into the stark reality of the present.

It was only after I had worked in government for a few years that I realised how our economic system was leading us into a dead end. After all, the Soviet Union had been developing along this same path for decades and the system seemed eternal and immutable. From the beginning, though, I did what I could to correct the most glaring absurdities: like the fact that Kazakhstan produced enough milk and meat to satisfy the needs of its own people, but had nowhere to process either of them, or that we had enormous amounts of raw hide but no tanneries.

The problem was not just the illogical nature of the system, it was also the way in which Kazakhstan was treated virtually as a colony. Of our exports to other Soviet republics in those days, only 12–15 per cent were finished products; the rest were raw materials or semi-finished. I tried, with local factory directors, to switch some of the resources from heavy industry to the production of consumer goods. It was an uphill struggle. Often we could not spend a single rouble without getting permission in advance from the all-Union government in Moscow. If we achieved anything at all, then it was only thanks to our persistence.

During those years, the real bosses of Kazakhstan and of the other republics were the central ministries in Moscow: the infamous ministry of medium machine building, which ran the Soviet nuclear programme, the ministry of non-ferrous metals, the ministry of energy and the ministry of defence. When they were drawing up their plans or working out how to exploit new sources of raw materials, they rarely took into account the interests of the individual republics. Of the billions of roubles which the ministries earned, only a fraction found their way back into the budgets of the republics. The Soviet Union was rare among countries in adopting such a colonial attitude to its own people.

CHAPTER FOUR

TWO SIDES OF PERESTROIKA

THE 11 March, 1985 – the day when Mikhail Gorbachev took over as general secretary of the Soviet Communist Party – will go down in history not just as the beginning of *glasnost*, literally openness, and *perestroika*, reconstruction, but also as the beginning of the end of the Soviet Union. Initially, however, there was little sign of the tumultuous changes to come. How slowly things were going was shown by the 26th Congress of the Soviet Communist Party, which was held almost a year later at the end of February 1986. Everything was much as it had been in the Brezhnev years, even down to the over-long, tedious boring speeches and the unanimous rubber-stamp votes.

Kazakhstan had been run for almost four decades by Dinmukhamed Kunayev. By then aged 74, Kunayev had so dominated the republic's affairs that his name was almost synonymous with that of Kazakhstan. On the morning of 16 December that year, his reign ended. A meeting was called of the Party's Central Committee. There was only one subject on the agenda – 'organisational questions', the Soviet euphemism for top personnel changes. The meeting lasted just 18 minutes and was stage-managed by Gyorgy Razumovsky, a departmental head in the Central Committee of the Soviet Communist Party. No one wasted any time on the usual long speeches. Instead they moved swiftly to the main business: the 'retirement' of Kunayev. In his place, as sole candidate, Razumovsky proposed Gennady Kolbin, the first secretary of the Ulyanovsk region of Russia on the River Volga.

Kunayev's departure was not a surprise to me. He had been to Moscow at the beginning of the month and when he came back he told me that he was stepping down. But it was only the day before the meeting, when Kolbin arrived in Almaty with Razumovsky, that we knew who was going to replace him. It was a strange choice. Kolbin had no link whatsoever with Kazakhstan: he had never worked there and was virtually unknown to the people. It was all the worse because of the hopes which Gorbachev had raised with his talk of new political thinking. This was old-style decision-making at its worst. But such was the mood of the times that no one thought of criticising the decision, let alone trying to oppose it.

Kolbin was elected unopposed and we were all sent back to work immediately afterwards. Razumovsky told us that all the necessary meetings would take place afterwards. The new Party boss clearly wanted to spend his time talking with the various members of the Central Committee of the republic's Communist Party.

Like most of my colleagues in the government, I was at my desk early the next morning; we knew that there was a possibility that we would be summoned to see our new boss. Our mood was grim; the events of the previous day had shown the indifference of the central authorities to the feelings and the opinions of the non-Russian republics and their inhabitants. The backlash came much more quickly than any of us had expected, however.

At around 9 a.m. I was told by one of my aides that demonstrators carrying banners were beginning to gather in the square outside the Central Committee building, which at that time was called Brezhnev Square. It was clear that they were protesting against the election of Kolbin. I immediately telephoned Oleg Miroshkhin, the second secretary of the Party, and Zakash Kamalidenov, who was a secretary in the Party leadership in charge of ideology. They confirmed what I had heard but told me to wait for further instructions. Officials from the Central Committee would investigate the situation.

However, I was determined to take a look for myself. I called my driver and we set off. Along the way, we saw columns of young people marching towards the square. I told him to stop the car. I got out and marched with them instead. By the time we reached the square there were several thousand people gathered there. They were already agitated, but the mood had not yet turned aggressive. One by one, speakers took the podium to voice indignation about the behaviour of the Moscow leadership. But they also urged the crowds to remain calm and demanded that someone from the Central Committee come and address them. I remember the banners which some of the people in the crowd were carrying: many carried portraits of Lenin on which were written, in both Russian and Kazakh, slogans such as 'We demand the respect of the Leninist principles of nationality policies,' 'No privileges for any nation' and 'Every people should have its own leader'.

I went inside the building and made my way up to the first secretary's office. Along the way I met a colleague who told me not to bother; Kolbin and the other senior Party officials had all gone to the ideology secretary's office, because he had a window overlooking the square. And there they all were, looking anxiously out of the window as more and more demonstrators gathered below them.

Kolbin had already summoned the Kazakh Interior Minister, the head of the republic's KGB and the public prosecutor. They were discussing what to do. The first information which they sent off to Moscow, to the Central Committee, the interior ministry and the KGB was distorted and panicky. The representatives from Moscow who had come down for the plenary meeting were looking at us suspiciously as if the whole thing was our fault. They took the initiative and virtually ignored our suggestions that we should try and analyse the situation carefully before taking action. Admittedly, though, the local leadership was also divided. The square was immediately cordoned off by police and special units from the interior ministry. The Almaty garrison of the army was put on alert.

It was decided that a few of us should go down to the square to talk to the crowd and try and calm them down. They chose four: Talgat Mukashev, chairman of the Presidium of the Supreme Soviet, Mendybayev, first secretary of the Almaty regional Communist Party Committee, Kamalidenov and myself. It was already about 3 p.m. by the time we went out. I noticed immediately that the mood had changed and the crowd had become much more agitated. Even so, we began to talk to them from the podium. At first they listened, although they whistled and began demanding that their representatives also be allowed to speak. People were starting to force their way on to the podium and I suggested that we let them speak. As expected, they criticised the appointment of Kolbin as humiliating and demanded that the decision be reversed.

Maybe, given time, we might have been able to win them over. But the matter was already out of our hands. Some members of the leadership, who thought they knew better, gave the order to drown out the speakers by playing loud music through loud-speakers which were set up around the square. This only antagonised the crowd, who began throwing lumps of snow, ice and rocks towards the podium.

Earlier, when we had been discussing tactics, I had suggested to the Party leader-ship that they should all go out among the crowd and talk to them, to try and establish some kind of dialogue with them. But both the people from Moscow and our local Party leaders refused. They insisted on standing up on the government podium and lecturing instead. It was typical of the attitude during those years; the leaders had their own rules and norms. Such behaviour would have been possible in the Brezhnev years, but times had changed. It was already more than a year since Gorbachev had come to power and launched his programme of *perestroika*. The hopes and new sense of self-consciousness which he had generated with his reforms could not now simply be re-suppressed.

That was the last chance that we had to influence things. Even the people in Kolbin's office were getting their orders straight from the Kremlin. I believe that the main reason that the representatives of Moscow tried to keep us from trying to control the situation in the square was that they knew that we could develop some kind of rela-tionship with the crowd, and were worried that we could somehow use it to our own advantage. Indeed, they became particularly worried when they saw the alternative names that the crowd were putting forward as their own choice for first secretary: Vasily Demidenko, Salamat Mukashev, Oleg Miroshkin, Nursultan Nazarbayev and other local members of the leadership – ethnic Russians as well as Kazakhs. Despite what the Moscow leadership would later maintain, this showed how wrong it was to accuse the crowd of being nationalists who objected to Kolbin purely because he was a Russian. The real objection was that he was an outsider. But this was not to stop the Moscow leadership using this argument against us. They treated myself and other members of the local leadership in a very insulting fashion.

Concern was growing in Moscow at what was happening. That same evening, an-other group of top Kremlin officials flew down to Almaty on a special flight. They were led by Mikhail Solomentsev, a member of the Politburo and Yevgeny Razumov, the first deputy head of the organisational department of the Communist Party's Central Committee. There were also senior officials from the KGB, interior ministry and the prosecutor's office. They moved quickly. In what was a direct violation of the law, Alexander Vlasov, the Soviet Interior Minister, was asked to send units of his troops to Almaty from various towns in the republic. With the police, they began an operation named 'Snowstorm' with the aim of neutralising what they described as 'the disorders in Almaty'.

The troops moved quickly against the demonstrators, using truncheons, sappers' spades and police dogs to break up the crowd. The final toll was grim: two dead, a young student and a policeman, and some 200 injured. There were also major infringements of the law when it came to the treatment of those who were detained: many were beaten severely and several were sent semi-naked out of the city despite the bitterly cold December weather. In total, some 8,500 people were either held temporarily in various kinds of remand centre or expelled.

These abuses continued when the court cases began against those involved – or often merely alleged to have been involved – in the protest. The prosecutors worked quickly and without much skill. In the end, some 100 people were charged over their role in the events, although 46 of them were 'rehabilitated' soon after. In a short time, some 800 young people were thrown out of the Komsomol, the Young Communist League, 270 were expelled from the various educational institutions where they were studying and hundreds more were fired from their jobs.

There have been many interpretations of the events of 1986. Initially, the 'disorders' were certainly not nationalistic in character and there was nothing illegal about them. They were begun by a group of workers who joined with young people to protest against the appointment of Kolbin. For many, his appointment was the last straw after years in which Kazakhstan was treated as little more than a colony. The protests were also peaceful and political in character: there were no demands to overthrow the state order or attacks on other national groups. However, the leadership was so steeped in the old, totalitarian ways that they were unwilling to sit down with the protesters' leaders and listen to what they had to say. They saw the protest as a direct threat to their power and reacted in the only way they knew, with force.

Most damning of all was the interpretation which was subsequently put on the events by the leadership in Moscow. In July 1987, the Central Committee of the Soviet Communist Party passed a resolution entitled: 'On the work of the Kazakh Republican Party organisation in the internationalist and patriotic education of the working people.' In it, the events of December 1986 were condemned as a 'manifestation of Kazakh nationalism' which was said to have been provoked by the sorry state into which the republic had degenerated.

The main target was the previous leadership under Kunayev which was accused of having created an 'unhealthy atmosphere' in the republic's socio-political life through its encouragement of bribe-taking, embezzlement and political patronage. Largely as a result, economic growth in Kazakhstan had slumped to the lowest of all the Soviet republics in the preceding decade, supplies of foodstuffs and other goods worsened and alcoholism had grown. Kunayev and his entourage were also accused of exaggerating their achievements and hushing up shortcomings to hide from the Kremlin quite how badly things were going.

The resolution was equally critical of the mistakes said to have been made in the implementation of nationalities policy and in the so-called 'internationalist and patriotic education of working people'. It was claimed that the republic's leadership had unfairly promoted young Kazakhs at the expense of Russians and members of other nationalities into key posts.

They were also accused of rewriting official Soviet history by playing down the Kazakh people's support for the establishment of Soviet power and daring to idealise their pre-Soviet past in scientific papers and works of literature and art and rehabilitating 'bourgeois nationalists'. This, it said, had led to a growth in 'nationalist manifestations' which were not curtailed in due time and indeed were hushed up or described as run-of-the-mill 'hooliganism'.

Just over a week later, Kunayev was stripped of his last official posts, losing his membership both of the Central Committee of the Kazakh Communist Party and of the presidium of the Kazakh Supreme Soviet.

Given Gorbachev's policy of *perestroika*, and his determination to change the way in which the Soviet Union was run, he was right to replace Kunayev. But the problem was the way in which he did it. Far from embracing 'new thinking', Gorbachev treated the leadership question in exactly the same way as it had been in the days of Stalin: just as they did with other republican and regional leaders, a small group in the leadership in Moscow selected Kolbin and then simply imposed him on the people of Kazakhstan. There was no attempt to take into account the views of the people. Gorbachev should have consulted the Kazakh Communist Party and entrusted them with the choice of a leader, ideally in a contested election. It should not have been too difficult to foresee the negative reaction to the appointment of an outsider like Kolbin.

Even if the criticism of corruption and misrule under Kunayev was justified, the solution chosen was certainly wrong. The emphasis which was put on strengthening the so-called 'internationalism' of the Kazakh people showed that the Soviet leadership did not understand the growing feeling of Kazakh national self-consciousness which had been behind the events of December 1986. Far from a manifestation of failure on the part of the local leaders, this was the natural reaction of the Kazakh people to decades in which the Soviet leadership had done everything in order to suppress their national identity.

However, it was impossible to speak openly and honestly and many people in our republic did keep silent. It was not until the convening of the first Congress of People's Deputies, in Spring 1989 – the first (nearly) democratically-elected parliament set up by Gorbachev – that the silence was broken and the first steps taken to set the historical record straight. Mukhtar Shakhanov, a deputy and secretary of the Board of the Kazakh Writers' Union, took advantage of the forum to propose the setting up of a commission to analyse the background to the December events. His proposal was supported by more than 100 deputies, among them Boris Yeltsin, the future Russian leader, and Andrei Sakharov, the Nobel laureate and human rights campaigner. But Shakhanov did not succeed in his goal of establishing a commission on a Union-wide level. It was set up only within Kazakhstan and contained many officials who had no real interest in uncovering the truth. It was also forced to include a group of USSR People's Deputies from Kazakhstan. Six weeks later, the members of the commission stopped their work following a decision made by the session of the Kazakh Supreme Soviet, the republic's parliament.

The problem was that it was only a preliminary commission and it did not have the necessary quantity and quality of specialists to do its job properly, nor did it have the necessary powers from the Kazakh Supreme Soviet. Also, the materials which were given to Shakhanov at first were full of twisted facts which in no way corresponded to what really happened. The question had to be tackled much more thoroughly.

However, events were moving fast. On 22 June, 1989 I was appointed leader of the Kazakh Communist Party and began to realise my own agenda.

My predecessor, Gennady Kolbin, tried hard to create the impression of being an energetic leader. But according to his style of work, the main weapon of administration was to hold meetings. Every week a meeting was held with regional officials of all ranks throughout the Party and the economic system. This constant pressure resulted in all sorts of unjustifiable decisions and programmes that were more declarative than anything else. For instance, declarations were made that Kazakhstan's housing shortage would be solved in five years, and that the food shortages would be overcome as soon as possible. Sometimes the campaigns were downright absurd. For instance, one way that the officials would try to carry out the food programme was by shooting wild animals and birds. All officials who did not speak Kazakh were ordered to learn the language immediately, and even Kolbin promised to present his report to the next Central Committee meeting in Kazakh. Kolbin was also a keen supporter of Gorbachev's ill-fated anti-alcohol campaign, with its establishment of so-called 'sobriety zones'. As a result, problems grew with drug addiction. So desperate were people to get high that they started using eau de cologne, toothpaste and shoe polish.

The anti-alcohol campaign highlighted the kind of dual morality which existed among government officials and Party bosses: one set of rules applied when they were among 'the people' and another when they were among their own kind. I witnessed a typical example of this in 1985 when Mikhail Gorbachev, who had just become the Soviet leader, visited the city of Tselinograd (which has since reverted to its old name of Astana), to attend a meeting of grain farmers. He was accompanied by an enormous entourage – the most prominent member of which was Raisa, his extravagant wife. All the leading figures in Kazakhstan were there, among them Kunayev, the heads of the republican ministries, and members of the local leadership. I was also there. After a long official meeting, we went to visit a few farms. It was only September, but it was already extremely cold. Later, we went to have lunch in one of the rooms in the residence belonging to the local Communist Party leadership. Although the alcohol campaign was at its height, I made sure that a couple of crates of wine had been placed ready in the room next door.

Raisa quickly began to dominate the conversation. Within a few moments, it became clear to me that she had an opinion on each and every subject under the sun, which her husband always took very seriously. We sat listening in silence as she expressed her categorical and often downright absurd opinions, until at one point she pointed out that Kazakhstan, although an agricultural republic, did not produce its own wine. I dared to contradict her. What's more, I said, although the leadership had declared war on alcoholism, this did not mean that we could not all taste a small glass of it. Kunayev kicked me under the table, as if to warn me not to stir things up, but I asked the waiter to bring in some bottles from next door. Everyone was very pleased to have a taste. However, you cannot expect men to make do with just wine, particularly when it was so cold outside and there was such good food on the table, so when a bottle of vodka suddenly appeared, nobody said no, not even Gorbachev, who was meant to be the leading 'abstainer'. This was just at the time they were about to launch their campaign to wipe out drunkenness from the entire territory of the Soviet Union.

To return to Kolbin, Gorbachev's protégé, it is true to say that everything that he did was little more than a political show which, as before, was largely directed and stage-managed from Moscow. His rhetorical and noisy campaigns brought no improvement to the economic situation and made no impression whatsoever on the population. On the contrary, there was a growing rumble of discontent within society. It became increasingly clear to the Communist Party leadership in Moscow that they would have to remove Kolbin – or else see him forcibly removed by his own people. And so they turned to me.

I was chosen as the new leader largely because of the way in which I had acted as Prime Minister – for the way in which I continually warned both the local Communist Party leadership and those in Moscow that *perestroika* was doomed to failure if no concrete plans were drawn up to put its ideas into effect. I had sent detailed reports to this effect to various different Party and government bodies and made speeches about it at plenary meetings of the Communist Party Central Committee and at the inaugural session of the Congress of People's Deputies. These included detailed proposals, especially on economic issues. All this drew me to the attention of the national leadership. It also helped that I had known Gorbachev for some time, was sympathetic to his ideas and had long pinned great hopes on him. Like many other Communists, I was still convinced that it would be possible to reform the Communist Party and its style of rule so that it would be possible to maintain the Soviet Union.

Gorbachev was determined not to repeat the mistake which he had made with Kolbin. I found out later that, before nominating me, the leadership consulted widely with officials in Kazakhstan about my suitability. It seems the majority spoke out in my favour. Although I was ambitious, I still thought hard before agreeing to have my name put forward for the post. In the end, I agreed, as this was the only way that I would be able to realise what I wanted to do for Kazakhstan and to break the ring of stagnation which surrounded the republic.

For this reason I did not really feel any sense of euphoria after I was elected first secretary. I knew that I had little time to carry out all the changes which were required. My priorities were essentially threefold: to strengthen stability and civil and inter-ethnic accord – a difficult enough task given the explosive situation in the aftermath of the events of Brezhnev Square; to work out and implement a programme of economic reform and to determine exactly what would be the division of powers between the republican authorities and Moscow.

Kazakhstan needed a period of calm and hard work. It was clear to me that the inter-ethnic tension had its basis in the socio-economic problems which Kazakhstan suffered in the late 1980s – an acute shortage of housing, food and consumer goods, as well as violations of social justice. For this reason, I set myself the task of tackling the housing problem and also trying to make Kazakhstan's socio-economic development more balanced.

But the infringement of the national dignity of the indigenous population was also a major contributory factor. Measures were taken to preserve and develop the traditions, customs and languages of all the peoples of Kazakhstan, but especially of the Kazakhs themselves. As part of this, the Supreme Soviet voted to make Kazakh the republic's state language. However, in order not to diminish the rights of the non-Kazakhs, Russia remained the language of inter-ethnic communication. I also spoke out firmly against any attacks on the Russian nation.

I was, at the same time, being drawn into the battle between conservatives and reformers which was raging in Moscow. I remember one Communist Party meeting in July 1989, just after I had taken over as Party leader, when Gorbachev shocked his critics by announcing that he wanted a purge of hard-liners from the leadership and their replacement by new blood. Instead, they turned on him and, in what was to be one of a series of escalating challenges to his authority, they said it was *perestroika* itself which was to blame. I was particularly incensed by their standard-bearer, Yegor Ligachev, who called for more curbs on the media and a crack-down on what he called anti-Communist groups. To their fury, I accused them of being afraid of democratisation and unable to free themselves of the traditional negative attitude towards dissent.

As a wave of national self-consciousness spread through the republics of the Soviet Union, so pressure grew in Kazakhstan for a proper assessment of what had happened in December 1986. For that reason, in January 1990, a second commission was set up by the presidium of the Kazakh Supreme Soviet. A month later, thousands of people demonstrated to demand full rehabilitation of the dozens of people who had been jailed and the more than 2,000 punished or dismissed for their part in the December events.

Despite opposition, the commission was able to complete its work. Its report was issued on 25 September, 1990, just over a week after the Kazakh parliament followed the example of most other Soviet republics and drafted a declaration of sovereignty in which it proclaimed the superiority of its own laws over those issued in Moscow.

The task was an extremely sensitive one, given that there were large numbers of people in the Communist Party leadership in Kazakhstan who wanted to continue to cover up the whole thing. In fact, such a cover-up did nothing to help the Party maintain its authority. Nor did it calm the people, as everyone in Kazakhstan, and not just those who had been standing in the square that fateful day, had been affected by the events.

I realised from the start that if the commission was to deal with this problem, then it had to be created in the most thorough and open way. It also had to be entitled to have access to all the official papers and to interview any officials whom it wished. However harsh its conclusions, this was the only way that it could do any good. I also sent a letter to the commission in which I gave my view of the reasons for the whole affair. I was pleased to see that the conclusion, when it came, was an objective one.

The Communist Party document of July 1987 had clearly pinned the blame on local hooligans and trouble-makers. In contrast, this one three years later highlighted the arrogance of the Kremlin. Through their powerlessness and reliance on force rather than on dialogue, Gorbachev and the Soviet leadership had managed to turn what had been a small and peaceful protest into an outbreak of mass unrest.

According to the report's finding, the decision to appoint Kolbin in the first place 'appeared an insult and was seen by the republic as a high-handed *diktat* of the Centre in matters concerning vital interests of the Kazakh people'. It found that the leadership had then merely compounded their errors: Vlasov's decision to send special units of the interior troops to Almaty from various regions of the country was illegal, while the anti-riot action taken by the security forces was accompanied by outrageous breaches of legality. Many people were detained without a specific order from the prosecutor and there were more breaches of legality during the judicial investigation which followed. Instructions issued by the Communist Party authorities to set up armed civil formations made up of workers and employees also added overtones of ethnic conflict to the events. 'The action by the Kazakh youth was not directed against any people,' the report said. 'It was the expression of a civic and political position.'

The commission was equally forthright in its criticism of the interpretation which Moscow had put on the events, condemning the 1987 report and the 'insulting accusations of nationalism' which had been directed against the Kazakhs. It also promised to find out and reveal the names of the Party and public leaders whose attitudes and specific actions had led to the use of force in suppressing what has been intended by the demonstrators as a peaceful political action.

Following on from the work of the commission, I passed a presidential decree in 1991 formally rehabilitating those who had been prosecuted for their part in the December events. From then on, 17 December was to be the Day of Democratic Renewal of the Republic of Kazakhstan.

A decade has now passed since December 1986. It would be wrong to say that the dramatic events of those few days are still a primary concern of the people of Kazakhstan. Far too much has happened in the intervening years. But what happened has not been forgotten, either. More than anything, those terrible hours in Brezhnev Square serve as a permanent warning of how the powers-that-be should *not* behave with regard to the people and to public opinion.

It is true that history teaches us a lot, but we do not always want to learn the lessons well enough to avoid repeating our mistakes. In 1985, we were told that it would take two to three years to restructure the economy. But even though Gorbachev correctly determined which general economic reforms should be carried out, it became clear later that he had not thought seriously about how to reshape the political system. Declaring democratisation and *glasnost* turned out not to be enough. No one seems to have realised what a terrible monster would develop out of these twins without radical reforms to accompany them.

At first there was a feeling that everything would change drastically for the better simply by eliminating a few aspects of the old system which particularly irritated people, and by letting the people openly express different opinions. But the things which we started to fight, like excess authority, unnecessary privileges, the stifling of criticism, bribery and corruption, turned out to be just the tip of the iceberg. They were the symptoms of the disease, not its root cause. That is why the Soviet Union went even deeper and deeper into crisis in the late 1980s and early 1990s. In a sense, we were seeing a repeat of what happened to Khrushchev's reforms of the 1950s and 1960s, although on a much larger scale because the changes this time were themselves far greater. In any case, it was unrealistic to believe that it was possible to turn the massive Soviet political and economic machine around in such a short period of time and achieve tangible results. Soviet history was full of examples of such a Utopian approach to the solution of complex social, political and economic problems. It had always failed.

By 1990, it had become all too clear to me that Gorbachev did not have any well thought-out plan for *perestroika*. He began by saying that we were learning as we went along, that life itself – as he always put it – was teaching us this or that. In reality, as I pointed out in a speech to the Party Congress in July 1990, the whole thing was little more than a process of trial and error. The economic situation, meanwhile, was getting worse. Inflation was getting out of hand, and the shops were becoming emptier. Living standards were worsening as the whole economy sank into a kind of primitive barter system. The people wanted discipline and firm leadership. Instead the country was sinking into chaos, marked by a series of bloody ethnic crises which erupted in the Caucasus and parts of Central Asia.

Gorbachev's fundamental error was his failure to listen to the Soviet republics' demands for economic independence. With the notable exception of the Baltic States there was no broad desire among the people in most of them – Kazakhstan included – for complete independence, but we did want greater freedom to control our own destiny. If Gorbachev had at once set out to provide maximum independence for the republics *within* the Union, then we could have avoided much of the subsequent upheaval. At least the federal authorities would not have literally collapsed under the weight of the economic mess which they had long been unable to handle.

How could Kazakhstan be helped if 90 per cent of its industry was under the control of the Moscow ministries? Unfortunately, our repeated demands for independence for our enterprises remained little more than a voice in the wilderness. The top leadership in the Kremlin had no understanding of how fed up we were with the high-handedness of the ministries in Moscow; nor the bitterness which we felt towards them for the rapacious plundering of our natural resources, the difficult social conditions under which our people lived, and the ecological tragedies of the area around the Aral Sea and Semipalatinsk.

For all Gorbachev's talk of restructuring, many of his top officials continued to behave in the old authoritarian way. Even such a highly important document as the plan for the country's changeover to a market economy was worked out without the involvement of the leaders of the various republics. It was all too hasty and feverish and reminded me of the desperate retreat of an army that had no previously prepared fallback positions. Where were all our scholars and entire institutions that had supposedly spent decades studying the problems of market economics? Even members of the Communist Party's Central Committee, the main policy-making body, only learned about the existence of the plans from the report of the Council of Ministers during a session of the Supreme Soviet.

What Gorbachev did not appreciate was that you need peace and quiet in order to learn. With each year of *perestroika*, the number of mistakes increased in geometrical progression. The most turbulent year was 1990 when it sometimes seemed as if the whole country were ablaze. Even then, it would still have been possible to save the Union. Strong action was needed, but Gorbachev was neither able nor willing to provide it. The stage was set for the dramatic events of the following year.

CHAPTER FIVE

THE END OF THE EMPIRE

I CAN still it remember it vividly. At 9 a.m. on the morning of 19 August, 1991, my wife rushed to wake me up. Although it was a Monday, I had gone to bed very late the night before and allowed myself the luxury of sleeping in. Her words were enough to wake me bolt-upright. She had just heard a report on the radio saying that Mikhail Gorbachev was sick and had temporarily stepped down in favour of Gennady Yanayev, his Vice-President. The announcer kept repeating appeals and statements by some emergency committee which she had never heard of before. The *coup* had begun.

I switched on the radio. It was just after 6 a.m. in Moscow and the announcer was reading out a series of statements by the so-called State of Emergency Committee. The Soviet Union was on the verge of breaking-up, it was said, and drastic measures were needed to pull it back together again. Gorbachev himself was too sick to do anything about it. Formally, the constitution gave the Vice-President the right to deputise for Gorbachev if he was unable to work. But as soon as I heard the name of Yanayev, one of the most conservative members of the leadership, I knew that something was wrong.

It was obvious that things were going to be bad for Boris Yeltsin, who had been elected President of the Russian Federation, the largest of the then Soviet republics, on a wave of popular support in June 1991, but they would also be bad for us in Kazakhstan. Like Yeltsin, I had frequently spoken out in favour of greater freedom for the various territories and republics of the Union, so that each would have the right to decide its own policies on economy, politics, foreign trade and foreign policy. None of that ever appealed to Yanayev and his allies. Now they had their chance for revenge.

I was tired because the previous evening I had seen Yeltsin off after a visit to Kazakhstan. We Kazakhs take our hospitality very seriously. I had invited him to come when we had met in Moscow the previous month, during President Bush's visit. Yeltsin had flown in to Almaty on 17 August, the Saturday before the *coup*.

The first day was taken up with the official part of the visit. I showed Yeltsin some factories and the historical museum, and then we went on to the Medeo, in the mountains, and to the museum of musical instruments. Normally, there is a little, informal concert at the end of tours of the museum. As the musicians were about to begin, Yeltsin called to one of his aides: 'Bring me my spoons'. So they brought some long-handled spoons and he joined in with the musicians. It was good summer weather, so I invited him to stay a little longer.

The next day we went to the city, and to the Panfilov State Farm, where we have a very good stud. We have a tradition of asking our honoured guests to name a horse. The name must consist of one letter from the father's name and one letter from the mother's. Afterwards we went to the Talgarsi Gorge, an enormous gorge up in the mountains near Almaty, where the mountain water flows like white foam. Several *yurts*, the traditional Kazakh tents, had been set up there. One was a giant dining room, in another there were bedrooms and in the third was the personnel. The water there was flowing very fast and there were jagged rocks, which made swimming very dangerous. But Yeltsin insisted. He said he loved swimming in the Moscow River in water which was just four or five degrees and described how he used to swim a little, then run, and breathe deeply and then swim again and so on.

So we let him swim and then we sat down together and drank a little vodka. I gave him a very beautiful black horse which he sat on and had his picture taken, even though he said he had never sat on a horse before. Some of my aides had to hold him to prevent him from falling off. Afterwards, a group of local girls sang folk songs.

In retrospect, it is remarkable that we could all have been so calm. While Yeltsin and I were relaxing on that summer day, the plotters in faraway Moscow were already sitting down to finalise their plans to topple Gorbachev. So secret were their plans that neither of us had any inkling of what they were plotting. For us, it was a day like any other.

By then, my relationship with Yeltsin had already become a close one. We had begun to work together from the end of 1990. Both of us had the aim of trying to stop the break-up of the Soviet Union, which we could see was coming. At the time, so many people were talking about independence and sovereignty, but both Yeltsin and I realised the almost certain consequences if it led to the break-down of the economic ties between the Soviet republics. The effect on the everyday life of the people would be disastrous. And that, in the end, despite all our efforts, was precisely what happened.

Yeltsin's plane was due to take off at 5 p.m. on 18 August, but it was delayed for three hours because of our celebrations. He finally left for Moscow at 8 p.m. Those three hours may have saved his life. According to one of his aides, an order had been given by the *coup* plotters to shoot down Yeltsin's plane as it flew past a military base near Aktyubinsk in western Kazakhstan. The soldiers were waiting at the due time to carry out their orders, oblivious of the identity of their intended victim. But the set time came and went. Since there was no further order from the *coup* plotters, when the plane finally did pass, it was able to fly on safely to Moscow.

After just a few minutes on that Monday morning, I had already heard enough of the statements of the State of Emergency Committee. I telephoned my office. The duty officer confirmed the radio reports but said that they still did not yet have a clear idea of what was happening. I tried to use the special government telephone circuit to call the Kremlin, but I could not get through. I knew I had to go to my office immediately to take control. But as soon as I stepped outside, I realised how serious things were. Every morning, my official car used to wait outside my home. For the first time ever it was not there.

The thoughts which went through my head would not be a surprise to anyone brought up in the Soviet Union: I thought of Stalin's purges of 1937 and again of the events after his death in 1953. Even the smallest thing out of the ordinary could be a sign. Shaken, I went back inside the house and picked up the special hotline which links me with my head of security.

'Who's there?' came the reply. And that was the special line which only I had the right to use.

It's all over, I thought.

I called my wife.

'Do we have anything at home which is at all compromising, which they could somehow use against me?' I asked. I had enough experience of working in the Soviet system to know how this kind of thing was arranged. They would search my home and produce documents and that would be it.

She could not think of anything, and neither could I. So I left. By now the car was there. There was a different driver from usual and he apologised. The delay had not been due to politics at all; it had been a simple mechanical problem.

As we drove along, I thought of the possible scenarios. Where would they stop the car? At one of the fixed police posts, perhaps? Or as I got out of it to go into my office? Instead, there was nothing. Everything went as normal and, soon after I got to my office, I received the first call of the day. It was Yeltsin.

'What's happening there, Boris Nikolayevich?' I asked.

'I don't know,' came the reply. 'But I think that this is a real *coup* and we must prepare ourselves for the very worst. I will take all the necessary measures.'

It was still only 7 a.m. in Moscow and I asked him where he was.

'At home in my *dacha*,' he said.

We discussed what he should do. I had successfully made it into work, but the situation in Moscow was very different. They could easily have detained him at any point along his route into the White House, where the Russian parliament had its headquarters. That is, if they expected him to go there at all. The big mistake Yanayev and his allies made was to believe that they could do everything according to the old Soviet rules. They thought that all they would have to do was to tell the people what had been decided by the leadership, the people would quietly accept it and then everything would go back to how it had been before. They did not appreciate the extent to which times had changed.

Yeltsin told me his decision. 'I will try and go there,' he said. 'You should keep following the situation because anything could happen. The main thing is that we should take a stand together against the State of Emergency Committee.'

The *coup* plotters did *not* try to prevent Yeltsin from going to the White House. It was their worst error, the result of which was visible on television screens across the world. When Yeltsin climbed onto a tank in front of the White House that morning and addressed the crowds, he immediately became a symbol of resistance to the illegal regime. By contrast, when Yanayev and his fellow plotters appeared at a televised press conference late that afternoon, they came across as nervous and ill-prepared. If there had not been so much at stake, the whole thing would have been a comedy.

That evening I addressed the Kazakh people on television and criticised the *coup*. I did the same, in even stronger terms, the following day, announcing that I was tearing up my Communist Party membership card and leaving the ruling Soviet Politburo in protest at the *coup*. My speech was not carried on either the radio or television in Moscow because they were both still in the hands of the plotters.

On the evening of 19 August I was called by one of Yeltsin's aides, Viktor Ilyushin, who asked me to try and do something to help. He said they were worried that the plotters were planning to storm the White House. Various Western leaders had called to offer their support and urged Yeltsin and the others to hold on. They said Yeltsin wanted me to use my influence to stop any attack. I agreed to telephone the Kremlin; the question was, to whom should I try to talk? They first suggested Yanayev, but I told them that I doubted whether he was really in control of the situation. We settled instead for Dmitry Yazov, the Defence Minister, whom I knew as being an honest and good person.

It was late and when I called I was told that he was asleep. They suggested I talked to Vladislav Achalov, his deputy.

'Is it true you are planning to storm the White House,' I asked.

He was indignant. 'Who told you that rubbish?' he asked. 'They are the ones who are firing at the tanks.'

Then I called Vladimir Kryuchkov, the head of the KGB.

'No, there won't be an attack,' he said. 'But people there are killing one another and we have to restore order.'

I warned him that if he did intervene and kill innocent people, then all the other Soviet republics would rise up against him. I had already spoken to the various republican leaders and knew their positions.

Then I called Achalov again and tried to persuade him to wake up Yazov. I told him that I knew Yazov well, our families even knew each other. Finally, in the early hours of the morning of 20 August, he agreed and we talked.

'What are you doing getting involved in this, Dmitry Timofeyvich,' I asked him. 'And what are you going to do now?'

'I don't know,' he replied. 'I have got myself caught up with these fools. What do you suggest?'

FIG. 9 The new national currency, the tenge, is introduced; the rouble is consigned to the past. In the banknote factory, May 1995.

FIG. 10 Looking at portrait of himself, whilst visiting an exhibition at a college
in the steel plant at Dneprodzerzhinsk, January 1994.

FIG. 11 Meeting in Washington with Vice-President Al Gore, February 1994

FIG. 12 With President Clinton in Washington, February 1994.

Fɪɢ. 13 With Prime Minister John Major outside Downing Street. London, March 1994.

FIG. 14 The Central Asian Union. On the path towards integration.
Meeting with the President of Kyrgyzstan, Askar Akayev
and the President of Uzbekistan, Islan Karimov, Kokshetau,
August 1994.

Fɪɢ. 15 With Pope John Paul II at the Vatican, September 1994.

FIG. 16 With Suleiman Demirel, Turkish President after signing the Agreement of Co-operation and Friendship. Ankara, October 1994.

FIG. 17 Kazakhstan receives security guarantees.
Left to right: Lukashenko (President of Belarus), Nazarbayev, Yeltsin, Clinton,
Kuchma (President of Ukraine) and John Major.
Budapest, December 1994.

'Pull your tanks out of Moscow,' I said.

In fact, I should have told him to turn them around and point them at the Kremlin, at Yanayev and the other plotters. Later, I spoke to Yanayev and proposed to him that I went to Moscow and acted as a mediator. He agreed. But when Yeltsin heard, he strongly warned me against it.

'They will arrest you when you arrive at the airport,' he said.

The presidium of the Kazakh parliament also insisted that my place was in Almaty, at the head of my people.

By the afternoon of 21 August, the third day of the *coup*, I had no more doubts that it had failed. The special government telephone lines were silent, as if they had been disconnected. I learned that Yanayev, Kryuchkov and Yazov had left Moscow by plane. But where were they going? To be honest, it never occurred to me that they would go to the Crimea and seek protection from the very President whom they had tried to oust. Moreover, CNN was reporting rumours that some of the committee members were already on their way either to Kazakhstan or Kyrgyzstan to seek political asylum. The theory was completely absurd. Even so, I ordered my civil aviation chiefs to check for any unusual traffic.

Nothing was known about the fate of Gorbachev, and that worried me particularly. I was convinced that the committee would stop at nothing to save their crumbling *coup*. For that reason, when the long-awaited telephone call came from Foros, where Gorbachev was being held, my joy knew no bounds. I even find it difficult to reconstruct in detail my conversation with Gorbachev, so powerful were the emotions which I felt at that moment. I will never forget, however, the unusually intimate tone of his agitated voice which made it impossible not to appreciate the enormous shock which this man had suffered.

Gorbachev thanked me for my support and asked me to express his gratitude to the people of Kazakhstan, who, during these difficult days, had shown their loyalty to the principles of freedom and democracy and to the lawfully elected state authorities of the Soviet Union. He also told me that the plotters, Yazov and Kryuchkov, as well as Oleg Baklanov, the former deputy chairman of the Defence Council, and Alexander Tizyakov, chairman of the Association of State Enterprises, were at that moment waiting to see him. Before meeting them, he had said he wanted to speak to Yeltsin and me.

We did not talk for more than ten minutes. After putting the phone down I was able to relax for the first time during those three days. The television in my office was still showing CNN. People came in and tried to talk to me, but I just sat there motionless, seeing and hearing nothing.

Then the thought suddenly struck me that I was the only one in Kazakhstan who knew for certain that the *coup* was really over. I looked at my watch; it showed 9.30 p.m. Kazakh television was showing *Vremya*, the flagship evening news programme from Moscow. That meant that almost everyone was now sitting at home in front of their televisions sets. It was an excellent opportunity and I left immediately for the Kazakh television centre.

No one expected me there, of course. When my aides found a free studio and asked the television engineers to interrupt transmission for a special broadcast, they protested that it was not possible. It was only when they saw for themselves that the President was sitting there, that they agreed to put me on air.

I did not speak for long. I just told the people of Kazakhstan about my conversation with Gorbachev, that he was in good health and had resumed his duties. I also passed on to them the thanks which he had expressed for the resolute stance which the republic had adopted during the *coup* and I congratulated everyone over the victory. After I left the studio they discovered that, in the rush, they had forgotten to make a video copy. I had to return to the studio and repeat the message which I had just broadcast. I did so with the greatest pleasure.

I was in high spirits when I got back to my office. Despite the late hour, almost all the members of the government and my aides were there. I have always made a point of never keeping alcohol in my office, but a bottle of champagne appeared out of nowhere and this time I did not refuse.

Some people are inclined to see the failure of the *coup* as proof of the conspiratorial incompetence of the organisers, who are presented as timid, hesitant amateurs. Look at Brezhnev, they say. Even he needed only one day to get rid of Khrushchev, despite the fact that the situation in the country at the time was far less tense and therefore less favourable for a *coup*. The difference lay in the people of the Soviet Union themselves. In October 1964 they were little more than silent observers of the struggle for power within the Kremlin. By August 1991, they were no longer prepared to accept the passive role which had been assigned to them. For decades, people had been paralysed by a kind of inbuilt fear which forced them to accept whatever their leaders said as being inevitable and beyond dispute. Those six years of *perestroika*, however painful, inconsistent and often contradictory, had not been in vain. The people had savoured their first breath of freedom. It had been enough for them to shake off the bonds of blind obedience and, once and for all, to reject any return to an anti-democratic, totalitarian regime.

You can only issue orders to those who obey, to those who are morally broken and deceived. That is precisely what made possible the purges of the 1930s and 1940s. I do not think that Yanayev, Kryuchkov and their allies would have hesitated, in certain circumstances, to use the methods of Yezhov or Beria. But these new self-styled saviours of the nation faced a very different country and a very different people and they cannot have failed to realise it. This explains their 'wait and see' tactics, their attempts to win over the leaders of the non-Russian republics and their fear of more radical measures which, had the political situation been different, they would not have hesitated to implement.

The timing of the *coup* was no accident. On 20 August, Gorbachev had intended to be sitting down in the Kremlin with me and other republican leaders to sign an historic treaty completely changing the way in which the Soviet Union was run. This new Union Treaty would have brought about a dramatic transfer of power from the centre towards the republics. Although only a minority of the republics had agreed to attend the signing ceremony, others were expected to follow later. I had always been a passionate supporter of the so-called Novo-Ogaryevo agreements which we had been working on during the previous months and which formed the basis of the Treaty. I scarcely delivered a speech, whether at a congress or public meeting or on television, without insisting on the need to sign the Union Treaty as quickly as possible.

It was the only way of saving the Union. To this day, I remain convinced of that, even though I can see now that I was overly idealistic in believing that forces loyal to the old order could ever have sat back and allowed the treaty to be signed. They saw that the Union Treaty would have been a death sentence for the powerful all-Union ministries in Moscow, which constituted the plotters' true power-base. They were right, but they were wrong to think that they could save themselves by staging a *coup*. On the contrary, it only accelerated the democratic processes already underway which they had tried so hard to stop. Their defeat was total.

However, even if the treaty had been signed, I doubt whether it would have resolved the political problem. Gorbachev had already left it too late; the crisis of confidence in our institutions had become too great and the authority of our state too small. In the end, he had been obliged to negotiate not just with the leaders of the full, Soviet republics such as Kazakhstan or Belarus, but also with the leaders of the 40 far smaller autonomous republics which lay within Russia, which were also now beginning to demand equal rights. 'We are not autonomous republics, we are sovereign,' they would say. This, in turn, led to a counter-reaction from many leaders of the Union republics, who feared that any increase in the status of the 'autonomies' would reduce their own. They had a point. It was all very well giving more powers to large and economically powerful autonomous republics such as Tatarstan or Bashkortostan, but there were many others which were tiny often artificial entities with no real separate identity. It would have been absurd for us all to have sat down together as equals.

Once Gorbachev was back in the Kremlin, we had to move quickly. It was not just a matter of removing and punishing the guilty men: with the old Soviet political system now well and truly dead, we also had to determine the shape of what would take its place.

Most of the personnel changes were agreed swiftly: Yazov, the Defence Minister, and Kryuchkov, the head of the KGB, had been arrested for their part in the *coup* and had to be replaced. Boris Pugo, the Interior Minister, shot himself. Many other less important figures had also been compromised. It was no secret that virtually all the new appointments were dictated by Yeltsin – a clear sign of the new balance of power within the country. It was on his initiative, for example, that Marshal Alexander Shaposhnikov was named the new Defence Minister. The main reason for choosing him was that he was said to have resisted the plotters and refused an order to bomb the White House. However, when we questioned Shaposhnikov about it, during a meeting of Gorbachev's presidential council, he was vague about whether such an order had ever actually been given. I was left wondering quite how heroic his role had been.

We also called in General Mikhail Moiseyev, the chief of staff, whom Gorbachev had named interim Defence Minister. Yeltsin was determined that he should go and on the next day, Gorbachev informed him that he was being relieved of his duties. Moiseyev stood up for himself. He demanded to know why he was being dismissed and insisted on being shown evidence. Gorbachev ignored his protests and got rid of him anyway. After that I decided to intervene and suggested that he be replaced with Vladimir Lobov, who was at that time working in Almaty as commander of the Central Asian military district. He was a good man who had shown his courage in Almaty during the events of 1986 when he had been under pressure to use soldiers to put down the students and had refused. By doing so, he avoided what would inevitably have turned out to be an even worse bloodbath than it was. After that we chose the others: Vadim Bakatin was put in charge of the KGB, Viktor Barannikov took over as Interior Minister. Alexander Bessmertnykh, the Foreign Minister, whose position during the *coup* had been questionable, was replaced by Boris Pankin, who was himself shortly afterwards replaced by Eduard Shevardnadze.

Determining a new political structure proved far more complicated. On 26 August, the Supreme Soviet, the Soviet Union's standing parliament, met for the first time since the *coup*. During a speech, I made it clear that from then on, Kazakhstan would not recognise any big brother. Relations between the former republics would be possible only on the basis of equals – at the most, a confederation.

After I sat down, Anatoly Lukyanov, the parliamentary chairman, who was himself soon to be forced out over his role in the *coup*, spoke: 'That's it. If that's the position of Nazarbayev, who is always in favour of integration, then that is the end of the Soviet Union.'

He had misunderstood my speech. I never proposed that we should split up completely. Indeed, at that stage, Kazakhstan had yet to follow the majority of the other republics which had already declared their independence. Instead, I was speaking about the desirability of a commonwealth or a union in which everyone would be equal and which was composed of sovereign states. But, at the same time, I insisted that the economy of the Soviet Union should remain united as a single unit. Perhaps more than any other of the leaders, I understood the extent to which all our economies were intertwined.

On 2 September, the Congress of People's Deputies, the full Soviet parliament, met for the first time since the *coup*. We sat there in the Kremlin day and night, but we all felt a certain powerlessness. Estonia, Latvia and Lithuania, the three Baltic republics, had already declared their independence, which had been swiftly recognised by the international community. For that reason they had not turned up. However, most of the other republics were represented. As I saw it, the main task now was to salvage what we could from the wreckage: to prevent the growing centrifugal forces from breaking the economic ties which had bound our republics together for decades. From this unified economic system a unified system of defence, foreign trade and foreign policy could follow.

For this reason, we decided to create a State Council and also an Inter-State Economic Committee. We signed the documents and I was given the task of addressing the congress in the name of Gorbachev and the ten republican presidents who signed. On my initiative, everything was firmed up. We named Silayev as head of the new Interim Economic Committee – *de facto* Prime Minister – with Grigory Yavlinsky, the young economist, as his deputy with responsibility for economic questions. We also began preparations of a treaty on economic union.

In the weeks which followed the end of the *coup*, I was in regular contact with Gorbachev both by telephone and at meetings in Moscow. I used to take the four hour flight there from Kazakhstan as often as once a week. The main issue was how to bring on our project for economic union. It was decided to finalise details at a meeting in Almaty on 12 October.

Of the twelve republics which remained in the Union, eleven dispatched representatives. The only one to stay away was Moldova. Even the three Baltic States sent along observers. The aim was to prepare and initial the agreement on the creation of the Inter-State Economic Committee and economic union. It was formed of some 25 detailed documents, such as the creation of a customs union, a unified economic space, a payments union, monetary union and so on. In short, there was everything to regulate the relationship between the various republics. Yavlinsky was left in charge of finalising the details and we agreed that the heads of state would meet again in Moscow on 18 October to sign the final version. Yavlinsky impressed me with the thoroughness with which he prepared the documents. Like me, he believed in the need to retain ties between the republics, and we have remained close ever since.

However, things did not turn out as planned. When the time for the Moscow meeting came, only eight heads of state turned up for the grand signing ceremony in the Kremlin's St George's Hall. Azerbaijan, Georgia and Moldova did not attend. More importantly, nor did Leonid Kravchuk, the Ukrainian President; in his place came Ivan Plyushch, the chairman of the republic's Supreme Soviet. But the republic did not sign on grounds that the agreement smacked too much of central control. It was immediately clear to us that what we had planned was not going to happen.

By now, Gorbachev was becoming increasingly desperate. He realised that nothing would come of our plans for economic union until we resolved the problem of political union. This was easier said than done. It had been hard enough reaching agreement before the *coup* when we held our repeated meetings in Novo-Ogaryevo to draw up the Union Treaty. The passions aroused by the *coup* had made it even more difficult.

Part of the problem was the growing nationalist sentiment in Ukraine and the determination of many people to rid themselves of that they saw as their republic's colonial status. The fundamental question was whether to set up a union, a federation or a confederation, but Ukraine would simply not agree to anything. Presidential elections were due in December of that year and Leonid Kravchuk, their leader, knew that he needed the support of the Ukrainian nationalist group, Rukh, in order to win them. But that meant that he was forced to follow an increasingly pro-nationalist policy in order to maintain his support with them.

There was also a shift in mood within Russia, which many of us in the other former republics found alarming. I remember well a public meeting in Moscow immediately after the failure of the *coup*, when a delighted crowd tore down the statue of Felix Dzerzhinsky, the hated founder of the forerunner of the KGB. What began as anti-Communism turned into a expression of Russian nationalism as they shouted '*Rossiiya, Rossiiya, Rossiiya*' – Russia, Russia, Russia. As I warned at the time, the euphoria of victory was turning into aggrandisement on the part of the victors and a distinct messianic note was audible in many of the speeches of the leaders. The Russian authorities were also assuming more and more of the prerogatives of the Soviet authorities. Gorbachev could not do anything without their permission. Neither, increasingly, could the other republics.

Even more alarming was the statement issued on 26 August by Pavel Voshchanov, Yeltsin's spokesman, warning that Russia had territorial claims against Kazakhstan and Ukraine, which it would raise if either of the two republics tried to leave the Union. When Yeltsin saw the damage which the remarks had caused, he quickly sent Alexander Rutskoi, his Vice-President, at the head of a large delegation, to both Ukraine and Kazakhstan to reassure us of Russia's good intentions. During his visit to Almaty, Rutskoi gave a press conference at which much was said about how good relations had always been between the Russians and the Kazakhs, and we signed a joint document confirming that Russia had no designs on our territory. However, the damage was already done: in those turbulent times, it was far too easy to make trouble by stirring up nationalist emotions.

It was not until October 1991 that we finally reached agreement to set up our economic union. A major reason for the delay was the strong dislike which some of the leaders felt for each other. Personal chemistry – or rather the lack of it – was every bit as important as policies or questions of statehood. All four of us, Gorbachev, Yeltsin, Kravchuk and I were brought up in the same school and saw things in the same way. While my relations with the others were good, there was no love lost between Yeltsin and Gorbachev. Of course, it was Gorbachev who had brought Yeltsin, then the first secretary of the Sverdlovsk regional Communist Party, to Moscow in the first place, six years earlier. Sverdlovsk was a large and powerful region, so Yeltsin's initial appointment as a head of department was not a very great promotion. And, although he later headed the Moscow regional Communist Party and was brought into the ruling Politburo, it was only as a non-voting 'candidate' member, not as a full member.

The thing that really rankled with Yeltsin was that Yegor Ligachev, who had only been head of the Party in Tomsk was a full member of the Politburo and he was not. It was against this background of resentment that these disputes in the Politburo began. The Communist Party heads of regions and republics were brought up expecting no one to answer them back. Yeltsin is the same. He likes to get his own way and does not like to lose.

Gorbachev had certainly not set out to slight Yeltsin. In those days, people were judged on their ability to work and Yeltsin was always a hard worker. When he was put in charge of the Moscow Communist Party he quickly went about establishing order and firing people. However, he went too far for some in the party hierarchy and they started pushing for him to be removed. At the end of December 1987 he was. From then on, he and Gorbachev were sworn enemies. There was little doubt that the energy with which Yeltsin fought his subsequent come-back was driven by the desire for revenge.

The most dramatic demonstration of how relations stood between the two men came during a session of the Russian parliament on the Friday after the *coup*, when Yeltsin started giving orders to Gorbachev in front of the deputies and in front of the people. This was a complete shock for Gorbachev. Yeltsin had saved him from Foros and Gorbachev believed that he would now support him. Instead, he humiliated him. Looking back, I often wonder how different the whole history of the Soviet Union would have been if Gorbachev had immediately made Yeltsin a full member of the Politburo when he came to Moscow.

We worked on through October 1991 and in November we met again. But again, we were unable to agree anything. I could see that the key issue was to reconcile Gorbachev and Yeltsin and I tried personally to help narrow their differences. I advised them to meet separately and try and get over their personal antipathy for each other on the grounds that the whole country expected it. However, Gorbachev's relationship with the Ukrainian leadership was almost as bad. It was becoming increasingly clear to everyone that there was no way that these three sides could agree on anything. The Ukrainians dealt him the *coup de grâce* on 1 December when they voted overwhelmingly for independence.

I had myself been re-elected Kazakh President the same day, and was determined to fight to save Gorbachev's planned Union of Sovereign States. But I warned my people that we must be ready for complete autonomy if the plan broke down.

A meeting was set for 9 December, at midday in the Kremlin. Gorbachev, Yeltsin, Kravchuk and myself were to take part.

I flew from Almaty to Moscow on 8 December but the day before I received a phone call from Yeltsin. He said he was planning to fly to Belarus so that he and that republic's leadership could help develop a common stance in their negotiations with Gorbachev.

After I arrived in Moscow I was told that Yeltsin was trying to get in contact with me. He was still in Belarus.

'Come over and join us,' he said when I picked up the phone.

'Why?' I asked

'We have just created a Commonwealth of Independent States,' he said.

'But we were meant to be discussing all these questions tomorrow in Moscow.'

'Come on, fly over,' he said. 'We can talk about it.'

For a moment, I almost decided to go and join them. They were all there at Byelovezhskaya Pushcha, Brezhnev's old hunting lodge: Yeltsin, Kravchuk, Stanislav Shushkevich, the Belarussian President and Vyacheslav Kebich, his Prime Minister. My plane was standing there ready, it would have been very easy for me simply to have flown there to see them.

'We're all sitting here, everything is ready, but we just need your signature,' Yeltsin insisted.

'Hold on a minute,' I said. 'You want me to sign just like that. I have to study it first.'

'We did not really read it ourselves,' he said. 'We just sat down and signed it.'

It was already seven or eight in the evening and I had the impression from the tone in his voice that they had already been drinking. Before committing myself, I asked if I could have at least a general idea of what they were agreeing.

Yeltsin then passed the telephone to Vyacheslav Kebich, the Belarussian Prime Minister, to try and persuade me. Kebich said the hunting lodge was not far from the city of Brest and he would come personally to meet me at the airport. 'The atmosphere here is all very warm and friendly,' he said.

I finally persuaded him to read me a little from the documents which they had signed so that I could get something of a flavour of the thing. When he did, I was horrified by how the federal authorities would disappear completely and how little provision was made for maintaining ties between the republics. Kebich admitted that it had not been planned that way, but that Yeltsin and Shushkevich had realised that Ukraine would not settle for anything else. And what kind of a union would it have been without Ukraine?

I was not entirely convinced. Of course Ukraine's position was important and had to be respected. But again at the heart of it was the personal antipathy between Yeltsin and Gorbachev. The main aim appeared to be to ensure that the unfortunate Soviet leader was completely deprived of his powers, that he was left with absolutely nothing.

At first, I was ready to go there. It was so close. But after they outlined the text to me, I knew that I had to refuse. I could not simply sign something like that without first consulting my advisors in Almaty.

When I asked them how they could justify their action, they said they were entitled to. When the Soviet Union was set up in 1922, it was done so by four entities: Russia, Ukraine, Belarus and Transcaucasus (which was later split into individual republics and ceased to exist). Therefore, as the three surviving members of the original four, they considered that they had the right under the constitution to dissolve it again. But between 1922 and 1940, another 12 republics had joined. How could they give themselves the right to dissolve the union without consulting everyone else?

It was clear that the Soviet Union was at an end and something would be needed to replace it. Such an agreement between the four was a solution: but I insisted that it had to be an open kind of pact which the other former Soviet republics would be free to join. It had to be fair. For this reason, I believed that we should tell the leaders of the other republics and Gorbachev what we were doing. The secret nature of the meeting did not appeal to me at all.

Before leaving the airport, I called Rutskoi. I assumed, that as Yeltsin's Vice-President, he would know more about it. He had not gone to Belarus, but was in Moscow. He angrily admitted that he did not have any idea what they were up to. Yeltsin had gone off with Gennady Burbulis, the first Deputy Prime Minister, and Andrei Kozyrev, the Foreign Minister. They were responsible for all the texts and had not told Rutskoi anything.

Gorbachev was also in the dark. He called me later to ask me if I had heard what Yeltsin and the others were up to in Belarus and wanted to know if I was still coming to meet him the next day. I spoke to him twice and he was clearly angry. In retrospect, it is clear that Gorbachev should have summoned a meeting of the Congress of People's Deputies, the supreme legislative body, in order to give its legal assessment of all this. But what kind of a session would it have been with Ukraine refusing to send its deputies there and Russia following suit?

The next day, we were all due to meet Gorbachev, but Shushkevich called from Belarus to say that neither he nor Kravchuk were coming. They said they were relying on Yeltsin to put across their joint position to Gorbachev.

The next day, I called Gorbachev at midday.

'So what do I do?' I asked. 'Go home?'

'No, come,' he insisted.

So I went to the Kremlin and we sat there, just the two of us. He already had the text of the agreement from the previous day in front of him. Five minutes later Yeltsin arrived.

Gorbachev immediately began to question him.

'So, you have agreed all of this,' he said. 'But what is going to happen about nuclear weapons?'

Yeltsin was silent.

'And what about the army? And what about the question of citizenship?'

Gorbachev kept on asking questions, like how Yeltsin and his allies were going to maintain economic ties and about the people whose families were split between the various republics. In the end, Yeltsin lost his temper.

'What is this, some kind of interrogation?' he asked.

They kept on talking anyway, but they did not decide anything. In the end Gorbachev merely said that he would study everything and they would meet again.

Afterwards I called the leaders of all four Central Asian republics and told them that we had to meet. The situation had become very tense. I did not want it to look as if it was my initiative, so I persuaded Sapurmurat Niyazov, the Turkmen leader, to hold the meeting in his capital, Ashkhabad, instead. Meanwhile, Yeltsin kept calling me, almost every hour, to find out what I had decided. He telephoned for the last time at around 9 p.m. and asked me if I was going to sign the accord. I told him that I could not do anything until I had consulted the Central Asian leaders.

On 13 December, we all met in Ashkhabad. Niyazov had a text in front of him calling for the creation of a Federation of Central Asia and Kazakhstan. I was all for caution. I imagined the situation: on one side there would be the Slav bloc of Russia, Ukraine and Belarus, on the other our Turkic-Moslem grouping. There was a danger that it could lead to some kind of open confrontation between the two blocs, especially because of the substantial Slavic population who lived in Kazakhstan. There was a danger that it would all play into the hands of the Russian nationalists.

Meanwhile, Yeltsin kept telephoning, urging me to persuade the others to sign. I refused and said he should talk to them himself. We sat there, the leaders of the Central Asian republics, until two or three in the morning and eventually we decided that we would join the Commonwealth of Independent States, but only on condition that we were all considered to be founder members and that Yeltsin, Kravchuk and Shushkevich came to Almaty on 21 December for us all to sign the documents. We also insisted adding a clause which said that the CIS should be set up in accordance with the law. That is, that the Congress of People's Deputies should have met and formally agreed to dissolve the Soviet Union. But it never happened.

The meeting took place as scheduled in Almaty on 21 December. It is not an exaggeration to say that the whole world was watching what was happening in the Kazakh capital that day. Never before had the city played host to so many foreign journalists, photographers and cameramen: more than 500 of them came for the summit.

After a brief discussion, the Treaty was finally signed. The feeling of relief all round was enormous. Admittedly, the leaders of the three Baltic States were not there, but we had never really harboured any illusions about them. The main thing was that we had done everything to prevent the Slavic and Turkic peoples of the former Soviet Union from becoming divided against one another. Within those few short days, we had taken one of the most momentous decisions of the twentieth century. The Soviet Union was dead. In its place were 15 fully-fledged independent states.

One of the major problems during these talks was what to do with Gorbachev: what role, if any, could he play in the new system which we were setting up? He was very passive during this period, as if he were in a state of shock. I think that, in his heart, he hoped that we would fall out among ourselves and have to call him in to sort things out. This did not happen. He and I used to talk quite often and I tried to explain to him that there had not been any alternative; that the only way out had been for us to agree on the creation of a confederation. He was the leader of a nuclear superpower and Commander-in-Chief of one of the most powerful armies in the world. But he gave up literally without a fight.

There was some talk of finding a post for him, but Yeltsin insisted that he had refused. If there was no USSR any more, then there was no place for Gorbachev. He wanted to leave politics and found his institute. However, the question remained about his status as the ex-leader. A meeting on the issue was set for 21 January, 1992.

There was no precedent for how to deal with him; all the leaders of the Soviet Union, except Khrushchev had died in office. As for Khrushchev, he had been re-moved and humiliated. Whatever Yeltsin's personal feelings about Gorbachev, I felt that it would be wrong of us to treat him badly. I said that we should not underrate his historical role and should not do anything which gave the impression that we were humiliating him, especially because of the popularity which he continued to enjoy in the West. We should be generous with him and not force him to suffer a repeat of Khrushchev's fate. He should be given what he wanted, whether state *dachas* or guards. Yeltsin thought differently.

We finally reached a compromise: Gorbachev was allowed to retire with dignity; but he had to tone down some of his more excessive demands, such as his initial insistence that he be given 20 personal guards.

PART TWO

BEYOND INDEPENDENCE

CHAPTER SIX

WE ARE THE KAZAKH PEOPLE ...

THE EVENTS which radically changed the face of the former Soviet Union are now part of history; since Kazakhstan won independence at the end of 1991, a transformation of the country's social, political and economic system has begun. The development of democracy, reform of property rights and the movement towards a market economy are the only way of lifting the economy out of crisis and of creating conditions conducive to the rise of a nation state in place of the old Soviet republic.

Our goal is clear; we want an open society and a democratic peace-loving state, which guarantees human rights and liberties, as well as political and ideological pluralism, a state with reliable defences and security and one which has a worthy, fully-fledged position in the international community of nations. The best way to achieve this is through a presidential republic.

Although Kazakhstan won independence in 1991, the old state structure of the Kazakh Soviet Socialist Republic remained. It quickly became clear to me, as it did to the leaders of the other republics, that there was a need for change. The question was how to achieve that change, since, as in the other republics, supreme power resided in the old Soviet-era parliament. In Russia, the struggle between president and parliament was eventually to lead to the bloodshed of October 1993 when Boris Yeltsin used tanks against his own parliament. From the beginning, I was determined to avoid such a conflict. Nevertheless, the old conservative forces were not prepared to give up without a struggle.

First and foremost was the need to draw up a new constitution. I assembled a group of legal experts from Kazakhstan and from abroad and set them to work. After several months they came up with a text which not only satisfied general democratic principles, but also reflected the specific reality of Kazakhstan.

My aim was to have the new constitution adopted in December 1992 in time for the first anniversary of independence on 21 December. As it was, parliament delayed, but they finally passed it on 28 January. It described Kazakhstan as a 'democratic, secular and unitary state'. One of its most contentious provisions concerned the language question, which had been one of the most heated issues during the last days of the Soviet Union. The result was a compromise intended to satisfy both the Kazakhs and the Slavs; Kazakh was made the sole official state language, but Russian acquired the status as the 'social language between people'.

Voting for a new constitution was only part of it; there was also the need to replace the old Soviet-era parliament. It was not just the nature of the institution itself, which was an unwieldy part-time body which met in full session only twice a year. The rules under which it was elected in 1990 were also far from democratic and its members, many of them workers and farm labourers, often lacked the experience needed to act as effective legislators. The whole system of Soviets – the Communist-era representative bodies from federal down to local level – was obsolete and fast becoming an obstacle to progress. Under the existing timetable, though, new elections were not due until June 1994.

Although some deputies continued to put up resistance, on 8 December, 1993, a majority finally voted to disband themselves. On the following day, they voted to dissolve all the local councils or Soviets and hand over management of the regions to local executive authorities.

In place of the outgoing Congress of People's Deputies, it was decided to create a new single-chamber, professional parliament of 177 people. Elections were set for 7 March the following year. In the intervening period, I was given the power to rule by decree, which I used as best as I could to push on with economic reform.

Around 700 people from various political parties or movements stood for 135 of the parliament's seats. Under the rules which were agreed by the outgoing parliament, another 42 were elected from the regions – two from each region. In the event, the majority of those elected broadly backed me and my policies, whether as members of the Union of People's Unity of Kazakhstan, a pro-presidential party, or as independents. However, there was also a small, if vociferous, minority who formed an opposition.

The elections were criticised by some foreign observers, including a small group from the Organisation for Security and Co-operation in Europe (OSCE). I am not ashamed to say that there was something to their objections. Inevitably, Kazakhstan's political culture had been deeply marked by the decades of Communist Party discipline and totalitarianism from which we had only just emerged. It was naive to suspect that we would overnight achieve the level of democracy of the United States, France or Britain. Nevertheless, the important thing was that we were moving in the right direction. Some 75 per cent of registered voters took part in the poll, opting for a wide variety of parties and movements. Importantly, the resulting chamber also reflected the ethnic make-up of the country, with around 58 per cent of the seats going to Kazakhs, and the rest to Russians as well as to other minorities such as Ukrainians, Germans, Koreans and several others.

From the start I made clear that the main task of the new parliament was to pass laws which would facilitate reform. In particular, we needed legislation which would allow for change in the banking system and taxation and which would help attract foreign investment. Yet many of the new deputies quickly showed that they had different ideas. Indeed, anyone who thought the parliament was going to be little more than a rubber stamp for the president and government was quickly disabused of the idea.

The first flashpoint came in May, when the new parliament passed a vote of no confidence in Sergei Tereshchenko, the Prime Minister. The deputies criticised the social, economic and legal policies of the government and said that while it professed free market policies, it was 'impeding and blocking' reform. In response, I carried out a minor reshuffle, but it was not enough. By that October it was clear that the whole reform process was foundering. There had also been accusations of corruption against some members of the government. Determined to bring reform back on track, I asked Tereshchenko to resign on grounds that he was no longer able to fulfil his responsibilities and replaced him with Akezhan Kazhegeldin, a pro-market economist, who was first deputy premier in the outgoing government.

However, it would be unfair to pin all the blame on Tereshchenko. As he complained at the time, the parliament kept trying to negate the government's economic strategy, by limiting its powers and interfering in economic and financial activities. Significantly, his resignation came as deputies were discussing one of the government's key economic reforms, namely raising the price of bread and of flour, which they had already turned down 15 times before.

Kazhegeldin quickly scored a first success where Tereshchenko had failed: after just two days in office, he managed to persuade parliament to accept the bread price increase, which was coupled with a compensation package to ease the pain for the worst off. The bread riots which many in parliament had apparently feared never took place. Although there were some protests, they soon died down.

Despite this initial success, parliament remained an obstacle to economic reform. Although relations never came anywhere close to the kind of conflict seen in Russia, I was becoming more and more impatient with what I saw as a delaying force. In December I appealed directly to the chamber to pass a series of reforms or risk jeopardising the country's recovery from economic crisis.

In the end, parliament did grudgingly pass a law on foreign investment and then, in March 1995, it passed a tight budget for that year. However, other key legislation was simply held up. Indeed in the course of one year it had only managed to pass a handful of laws which were necessary for the transformation of the country. This was at a time when economic reform was being choked by the lack of a civil and tax codex, and of laws on bankruptcy, foreign investment and so on. In a major obstacle to reform, the deputies also voted against land privatisation and against giving the Russian language equal status to Kazakh.

None of this was because the members of parliament were incompetent or were deliberately sabotaging our work. It was more a question of the lack of experience of parliamentarianism in our country and the poor legal preparation of the deputies. They were drowning in details and trying to deal with less important problems while neglecting the most important ones.

However, they were also opposed to key elements in my programme, namely their voting against allowing private land ownership and against giving equal status to Russian and Kazakh as official languages. At least on the land question, surveys showed that they were out of touch with the mood in the country: a clear majority of people, both Kazakh and Russian, was in favour of private ownership.

Surprisingly, the crunch came not over economic reform but over the manner in which parliament had been elected. After the poll, one of the unsuccessful candidates went to the constitutional court to complain about the way in which the contest had been conducted. On 6 March, 1995, the eve of the first anniversary of the elections, the court ruled in her favour. The decision affected more than one candidate. The court ruled that the election authorities had failed to comply with the rules on a number of points. If followed through to its logical conclusion, the result was clear: the entire parliament had been elected under false pretences.

My initial reaction was to veto the ruling on the grounds that it was unfounded and that, strictly speaking, it did not come under the court's jurisdiction. My main concern was political stability which was hardly going to be helped by such a ruling. However, after the court met again and reconfirmed its judgement, I realised that I would have to change my mind. On 11 March, a Saturday, parliament met in an emergency session. Its members appealed to me to solve the crisis simply by amending the constitution and adding a clause which would allow parliament to overturn decisions by the court and suspend the court from working. I refused. The fact that parliament was illegal had received its final judicial confirmation and I knew that I had to follow the constitution to the letter.

That evening, at a hastily convened news conference, I announced that I was dissolving parliament. I also formally appointed a new caretaker government to be headed by Akezhan Kazhegeldin, the Prime Minister, and a core group of his senior colleagues, including the Foreign, Finance, Interior and Defence Ministers, all of whom were to keep their jobs. In a sign of the extent of the crisis, I postponed a visit I was about to pay to Indonesia and Australia.

The decision I announced that Saturday was one of the most difficult of my career, not least because of the resistance which many of the members of parliament put up against it. Two days later, some 70 of the total 177 lined up behind Olzhas Suleimenov, the poet and anti-nuclear activist, refusing to have the chamber disbanded. Small, if noisy, protest meetings were called, and a couple of dozen of them staged hunger strikes. But they had little real popular support, and their revolt quickly fizzled out. A planned meeting of an alternative assembly set for 16 March failed to take place and by the end of the week the last of them voluntarily left their offices.

Many commentators abroad and even within Kazakhstan were critical of my actions, accusing me of dissolving parliament and doing so for my own ends. This was not true; indeed, according to the constitution which was then in force, the President did not even have the right to dissolve parliament. I merely bowed to the decision of the constitutional court. What could be more democratic than that? Indeed, if I had done the opposite and put pressure on the constitutional court and succeeded in making it change its position, I would have been criticised as well.

Essentially there were two questions: did the fact that the mandates of some deputies were ruled to be illegitimate mean that the parliament as a whole was illegitimate? And if so, who was entitled to take over legislative decisions? Strictly speaking, I did not take any extra powers for myself; they had already been delegated to me by the previous parliament in 1993 when there had been an analogous situation. The court's answer was clear: the mandates of the deputies were unconstitutional and the law temporarily granting the presidency extra powers continued in force.

I went out of my way to avoid any signs of vindictiveness towards the former deputies. Immediately after the court's decision, we created a commission to find work for those who had suddenly lost their jobs; each case was examined in detail. In the end it was only a minority who continued what they liked to describe as a political struggle. That was their affair. By doing so they demonstrated that their priority was not their responsibility to voters or a matter of principle, but rather their own personal interests.

The court's decision was totally unexpected. However, this did not stop me making use of it to do what I believed best for the country. There was no point in rushing into a re-run of the elections. The outgoing parliament had failed Kazakhstan in many ways. Electing another body under exactly the same rules would simply produce the same kind of brake on reform as its predecessor. We needed time for reflection, time to complete the overhaul of decision-making process which we had begun with the first post-Soviet constitution of January 1993.

As I had come to believe, one of the main elements in this was strengthening the role of the presidency. Working out how best to do that was a complicated question. In the meantime, I decided to give a further boost to the reform process by ruling by decree, under powers which had already been granted to me by the old parliament. What began as a crisis could be turned to the advantage of the republic.

When considering the former Soviet republics, many of which were torn by internal conflicts at the time, I was reminded of the parable about an old nomad. The man died and his sons decided to share out his possessions equally among themselves: his sheep, his camels, his horses and all his furniture. Each one was happy with his share, but suddenly they remembered their father's copper saucepan – who was to have it? They could not divide it up and, as no one was prepared to give in, they began to fight over it. After a long struggle, they finally decided to make peace. But by then they had lost everything; all their sheep, horses and camels had wandered away. The only thing left was the copper saucepan itself, but nobody needed it anymore, because they had nothing to cook in it.

We do not want to make the same mistake in Kazakhstan. We do not want to waste all our country's economic and intellectual potential in conflicts, whether inter-ethnic, religious or of any other sort; our main aim should be instead the strengthening of stability. It was for this reason that I supported proposals to create a new advisory body, the Assembly of the Peoples of Kazakhstan, which was set up just a few days before the court issued its historic ruling.

The assembly is a unique body which has the aim of providing a forum for the views and interests of the many ethnic groups which make up the population of Kazakhstan. Grouping the most influential and authoritative members of the various communities, it concerns itself with the most important issues affecting the country, especially those relating to nationalities policy. Although its decisions are only of a consultative nature, they help the President to formulate both current and long-term policy.

When its members gathered during its first session, they quickly came to the conclusion that the only way to prevent a repetition of the political crisis which had engulfed the country was to strengthen the powers of the presidency. As an important first step towards this, they proposed extending the current presidential term until December 2000.

Given my own thinking on the subject, I was necessarily sympathetic to the proposal. 'We hear cries that there will be a dictatorship,' I said in my speech to the assembly. 'Yes, dictatorship will come, but it will be a dictatorship of the constitution and of the law. The danger of real dictatorship comes instead if chaos and anarchy are created under the guise of democratic slogans. Then the people will start to call for a firm hand.' I moved quickly. After confirming with constitutional experts the legality of such a move, I announced the next day the holding of a nation-wide referendum on extending my term from December 1996 until December 2000. I also set up a central electoral commission to oversee the vote. Polling was set for 29 April, 1995.

In so doing, I was taking on myself full responsibility for the continuation of economic and political reform in Kazakhstan. Abandoning it half-way would have plunged the country into chaos and put under threat everything which we had achieved. Some people were critical, accusing me of seeking too much power for myself. It was not true. As I said at the time in a speech to a trade union congress, I was not holding the referendum for myself. It was for the sake of political stability and for the majority of people who did not want to see a repetition on Kazakh soil of the kind of inter-ethnic violence seen in the various trouble spots of the former Soviet Union.

When the poll was held, the country's nine million voters were asked one simple question: 'Are you in agreement with extending the authority of the President, elected by the people, until December 2000?' The result exceeded even my expectations. Turnout was well over 90 per cent, and, of those who voted, just over 95 per cent backed my proposal.

I took the vote essentially as one of confidence in my goal of creating a stable, multi-ethnic Kazakhstan. If people wanted to judge me, then they would have to do so on the basis of the practical steps which I took towards achieving this goal.

The result also gave me the mandate I needed to push on further with my programme of reforms. The following Friday, 5 May, I announced a second referendum, for that August, changing Kazakhstan's constitution and paving the way for elections to a new parliament. The aim was to create the most democratic possible document in the post-Soviet region. A preparatory conference was set for that June. Shortly afterwards, I set off on my first state visit to South Korea.

The draft was formally launched on 30 June. It was decided to put it up for a month of public discussion before a referendum set for 30 August. Many experts from Russia, France, USA and elsewhere were involved in the creation of the new constitution whose main goal was to create the constitutional foundations for a strong, independent state. The style of rule was deliberately presidential, although an important role was also given to the bicameral parliament – a lower house, known as the Mazhilis, composed of 67 directly-elected members and a 47-seat Senate. Under the new rules, the President would choose the Prime Minister and, if the parliament objected, he could call fresh elections. The same applied if parliament passed a vote of no confidence in the government. The President also had the right to appoint seven members of the Senate.

However, in a significant limitation on his power, he did not have the automatic right to initiate legislation, although parliament could award him special law-making powers for up to a year by a two-thirds majority at a joint session. Another safeguard was that if the President did wrong, he could be impeached provided that there was a three-quarters majority of a joint session of parliament. Although powerful, the President would be no dictator. In fact, he would actually enjoy less power than his French equivalent.

Some modifications were made to the constitution in the course of the month of public debate which followed. One of the most important changes made to the final draft was the establishment of a six-member constitutional council to replace the previous constitutional court, with two members established by the President, two by the Mazhilis and two by the Senate. This allowed the council to be above politics, independent and free of outside pressure. Nevertheless, the main lines of the document remained intact.

The main feature of the constitution is that it gives a firm and clear solution to the most important social problems which have concerned the people of Kazakhstan all these years: the problems of language, of property and of citizenship. To this end, it also contains an important concession to the substantial Russian-speaking population, promoting Russian to an official language which would be equal in practice, if not in name, to Kazakh.

In our country, with its 17 million people of various nationalities, ages, professions and outlooks, there cannot be a single view of our constitution. There will necessarily

93

be differences of opinion and some elements which displease certain people or groups. This is inevitable in a democratic society. We should bear in mind one question: does this constitution provide us with the prospect of peaceful, stable life for the state and for each family which lives in it? I am convinced that it does. It was precisely this feeling of responsibility for the fate of the people of Kazakhstan which motivated me when I took such an important step as revising the constitution in the first place.

The result was almost as encouraging as in the April referendum: turnout was 90.58 per cent, with 89.14 per cent of those who voted backing the new constitution. With this important result behind me, I then set 9 December that year as the date for what was to be the third and final step in the constitutional reform process: the holding of elections to the new parliament.

A total of 278 candidates stood in the election for the lower house, most of them from six parties and several social organisations, but also with more than 100 independents. The largest number of candidates was put forward by the pro-presidential Party of Popular Unity, which was founded in 1995 and headed by Akhan Bizhanov, one of my advisors. Its main platform was one of inter-ethnic harmony, stability and support for presidential reforms.

Other groups which stood included the People's Congress, the Communists and Socialists which formed an open opposition. Although there was no restriction on parties as such, it was decided to elect candidates as individuals and not on the basis of party lists. There was also no mention on the ballot papers of the candidates' party affiliation. This was deliberate. The Russian Duma elections of December 1993, with the huge gains they gave to the Communists and Zhirinovsky's Liberal Democrats, had shown us how dangerous and destabilising this could be.

As for the Senate, 40 of the candidates for the upper house were elected by regional authorities, two from each region, from each city of 'republican importance' (as the major cities are called), and from the capital.

The new parliament convened for the first time on 30 January, 1996. The biggest bloc was the Party of Popular Unity. In my inaugural speech I warned deputies not to repeat the mistake of their predecessors and to move decisively towards reform. The main condition of democracy was stability, I told them. I reminded them of past parliaments whose internal divisions had ultimately opened the way to upheaval or revolution, whether the Russian Duma of 1917, the German Reichstag which allowed Hitler to come to power in 1933, or Russia and the stormy events of 1993. For my part, I pledged to do everything to ensure that the parliament worked for its full term.

At last, four years after independence and 10 months after the disbanding of the old parliament, freedom of speech and political pluralism had been finally and irreversibly established. The new parliament is not only more compact than its predecessor, it is also made up of competent deputies, who demonstrated their political maturity in June 1996 by backing the Kazhegeldin government in a vote of confidence when it asked for a free hand to introduce economic reform. Thanks to its new powers, the government has also begun to act in a far more decisive and effective way. Importantly, we have been able to do this without slowing the democratic transformation of our society.

In adopting a new constitution, one of our main concerns was to strengthen Kazakhstan's image abroad. This was all the more important because of the growing interest which businessmen from all over the world are showing in the country. Judging by discussions which I have held with representatives of foreign companies, we succeeded in our task: people are impressed by the supremacy of law in Kazakhstan, the civil peace and the good relations between the different ethnic groups. This, in turn, means that much-needed foreign investment will continue to flow into the country. This is the important thing; not some criticism voiced by those far away who know little or nothing about the reality of life in Kazakhstan.

Some talk of a Western model of democracy or an Asian one. I do not believe in such a distinction: democracy is democracy. You either have it or you do not. Its basic elements are universal. The real distinction is instead between a democracy which has already been created and perfected, and one which is still in an embryonic stage. For that reason, it is still far too early to compare the current political situation in Kazakhstan with that in, say, Britain. They have had centuries in which to refine concepts of individual liberty; so far we have only had a few years. Kazakhstan's democratic institutions are like infants taking their first, faltering steps.

For the same reason, it is misleading to compare the political parties of Kazakhstan, or any of the former Soviet republics, with those in the advanced Western democracies, which have built up their electorates – and identities – over the course of decades, or even centuries. Ours have only just been created. Many of our politicians, too, are little more than demagogues who are ready to make all sorts of rash promises merely in order to win power.

However, these are little more than growing pains. Creation of a multi-party system will deepen the transition to democracy, promote the consolidation of our multi-ethnic society and produce a new generation of political leaders. With time, the parties will come to reflect the differing interests of the various social groups, which depend in turn on their occupations, the property they own and so on.

Nevertheless, Kazakh law also makes clear that political freedom does not mean license: in particular, we decisively reject political parties and organisations which are based on national, class or religious intolerance. We will also take a tough line against those which pose a threat to the constitutional system and the territorial integrity of our sovereign state.

The emergence of a genuine middle class will play an important role in the realisation of radical reform. Such people, characterised by their moderation and caution, form the backbone of any democratic system. Within the CIS, such a middle class is only now beginning to be formed. As it grows, it will help bring stability to economic development in particular and to society as a whole. It is this class which will allow society to overcome the old Soviet 'dependency complex', the feeling that the government is there to help you whenever you fall into economic difficulties. The key to the development of such a class is acceptance of the right of citizens to be property owners. We must also explicitly reject any repetition of the forced confiscation of property which has happened more than once in the Soviet Union during our memory.

Nevertheless, the state still has an important role to play, especially in the transitional period when the living standards of the population are going down rather than up and the gulf between rich and poor is growing. Many people will be unfamiliar with the working of the market; many more will be without adequate practical skills to allow them to adapt easily to the new conditions. We should therefore understand why many people have a negative attitude to the reforms and work hard to convince them why they are necessary. Without this, reform will simply not succeed.

For this reason, the state will retain its function of regulating the socio-economic process, albeit indirectly, in order to strike a balance between economic freedom and purposeful action by the state. The strengthening of presidential power is part of this. For, without it, far-reaching economic reform is impossible. The state should be perceived by citizens as a capable guarantor of rights and law and order.

Closely linked with this is an increase in the legal consciousness of the people, whether as individuals or as part of businesses – or indeed, as members of the government. We must turn on its head the old Soviet principle of the supremacy of politics over law. In a truly democratic state, no one – not even the President – can be above the law.

Democracy is knocking at the door of Kazakhstan. But we have to prevent it blowing through like a tornado. Each country has to decide to do things in its own way.

There can be no such thing as 'democracy by decree'. At the moment, in Kazakhstan, it is the state which is the guarantor of economic reform, of liberalisation of the economy and of broad-ranging privatisation, even if the latter means that the state will lose its monopoly and is literally cutting away the branch on which it is sitting. For that reason, the referendum on increasing the powers of the President and extending the presidential mandate must be seen as forcing the pace of reform and of the other positive processes underway in Kazakhstan.

Our main achievement over the last few years has been to create the legislative base for reform, in particular for passing laws which allow for the creation of a market economy. The vexed question of private land ownership has been solved. We have also made great progress in reforming the system of law and order; we have separated the investigators' service from the procurator and the courts: we have finally broken with the legal system inherited from Stalin's show trials of the 1930s. We have greatly strengthened the legal possibilities of the *militsia* (the police) and have created a special group with the task of clearing the country of organised crime groups; in the course of six months, they have managed to round up most of them. Although the level of crime remains a major problem, we have at least made some progress in reducing it.

In addition, we have carried out a major reform of the executive, which was vital for bringing the country through the current, transitional period. Under the terms of the new constitution, the President himself forms the government and names the representatives of executive power from top to bottom. However the local councils or Maslikhati, (which were known in the Communist times as Soviets) have the right to stage no confidence votes in any heads of the executive, whether of the district, town or region. A two-thirds vote is required. In such a case, the President must automatically remove such an official from his or her post. Further controls are provided by the strict separation of powers between the parliament, government and the legal organs. If any of them infringe the constitution, then they can be made to answer for their actions.

One of the most important decisions which I have taken since independence was to move the capital from Almaty to Astana[1] just under 1,000 kilometres to the north.

When parliament approved my proposal in July 1994, a lot of people thought that it was a hasty decision. On the contrary, I had been weighing it up for years. There are a number of reasons, chiefly that Almaty has simply run out of space to expand. Almaty was built for 400,000 people. Today, it has grown to one and a half million. If it is to remain the capital, then it must expand further, but the ring of mountains which surrounds the city make further growth impossible. Despite their beauty, the mountains also affect the quality of air, helping to make Almaty's ecological situation among the worst of any Kazakh city.

That is not the only problem. Geographically, Almaty is in the wrong place, in the far south-east corner of the country, near the border with China. This is bad not only from a strategic point of view, but it also has the effect of turning the city into a place of bureaucrats, cut off from the real life of the republic, from its industrial and agricultural centres. To fly to Almaty from the west of Kazakhstan, let alone from Russia, costs a fortune. All this might not be so important for a developed country where many of the functions of government are in the hands of the private sector, but given the enormous transformation which is going on, the President and government are obliged to keep a tight hold on the pulse of the country.

Nor is there anything accidental about the choice of Astana. During Khrushchev's time, Tselinograd, as it was known in those days, was specifically developed as the future capital. Lying on the cross-roads between the main north-south and east-west

---

1   The city was known at the time as Akmola, but its name was often mistranslated and so, in 1998, I changed it to Astana.

lines of communication in Kazakhstan – and indeed in the former Soviet Union, it is open for further expansion. Moving the government there does not present many problems. Within the grandiose buildings of the Tselinograd Regional Communist Party alone there is room for the entire presidential apparatus, government and parliament of the country!

Of course, the project has been criticised. Some have pointed out the cost of the move. However, they should set this against the even greater cost of expanding Almaty. Indeed, the move will give a great stimulus to the development of the country. We have already received requests from companies interested in investing in the new capital, including one group which wants to build a US$200 million business centre there. The company is proposing building and running it on its own, without demanding a cent of public money. Another Western financial group wants to build a new airport and terminal in Astana and run it for five years. Again, we would not have to pay anything. South Korea has also shown interest, although some doubts have been cast over its involvement by the country's current economic crisis. There are many more such examples.

There is also understandable concern about what will happen to Almaty once the government has left. We are hardly all going to fly off and leave it to its fate. It will continue to develop as the main financial-economic, scientific and cultural capital of the country. We also plan to give it the special status of a free economic zone, with tax privileges and other such benefits. Entrepreneurs there will be given *carte blanche* to create more jobs in industry as well as developing the region's enormous potential for recreation and tourism.

Many people predicted that we would never make the move and that it would remain little more than a bold idea. On 19 December, 1997, less than three years after my initial announcement, I was able to prove such critics wrong. At a joint meeting of the Kazakh parliament and the cabinet at the new presidential residence in Astana, I read out a statement formally declaring the city as the new capital.

'For the first time in its dramatic twentieth-century history Kazakhstan has made its own decision on the capital,' I said. 'Kazakhstan is a Eurasian country and Astana is one of the geographical centres of Eurasia.'

CHAPTER SEVEN

CURRENCY AND ECONOMICS

THE aircraft were ready: four giant Ilyushin-76 transport planes climbed from Almaty in mid-October 1993 and set their course for London. Their secret mission: to collect tonnes of brand new tenge bank notes which were to be distributed across Kazakhstan in place of the discredited rouble. We had only a few weeks in which to complete the operation; the new currency was to be introduced on 12 November. But we had no choice. The alternative was the ruin of our economy.

It was not a decision which we had taken lightly. During the Soviet years, the rouble had been firmly established as the currency of the whole Soviet Union. Even after the collapse of the Union at the end of 1991, there were many people, including myself, who wanted it to remain that way. More than 70 years of Soviet rule had ensured that the economies of the former republics were tightly bound together. Indeed, this was one of the central goals of what used to be called the socialist division of labour. Raw materials were taken from one end of the Soviet Union, sent thousands of kilometres for processing and then transported another several thousand to their markets. No one took any notice as they crossed the borders of the Soviet republics.

Often, it was a matter of logic: many raw materials were situated a long way both from those who could process them and the end users who would buy them, and so they had to be transported. Often, though, it was purely political: economic links were used deliberately to bind together the Soviet republics on a political level. It also served as an instrument of 'Russification': factories were built in areas where non-Russians were in a minority and then tens or even hundreds of thousands of Russians were encouraged to settle there in order to dilute them. These incidentally, form the basis of many of the Russian minorities of today both in Kazakhstan and elsewhere in the former Union.

Some mistakenly compared the relationships between the non-Russian republics and Russia to that between the countries of Eastern and Central Europe and the Soviet Union. This was not the case. Poland, Hungary and the others all had separate economies, albeit ones which were linked to one another. The Soviet Union, by contrast, was *one* single economy.

No Soviet republic was more integrated into this whole than Kazakhstan; a result not just of its size but also of its geographical position, straddling the border between Russia and Siberia to the North and the republics of Central Asia to the South. An overwhelming percentage of our enterprises were 'Union-level' ones: they were controlled by the all-powerful ministries in Moscow. The majority of our industrial production also went to Russia and the other republics. The most dramatic symbol of this inter-dependence are the oil and gas pipelines, which run North–South rather than East–West. As a result, the crude oil from our huge reserves, which lie in the west of Kazakhstan, must be sent northwards to Russia for processing, while the refined oil which we use in Almaty in the East, comes from refineries in the Urals, in Russia. Hence the absurd situation in which citizens of one of the largest potential oil producers in the world must frequently put up with shortages of petrol for their cars and bottlenecks in fuel-supplies for their aircraft.

Whatever the shortcomings of the old system, we had little choice after independence but to live with it, at least in the short term. Re-orienting industry will be a costly process which will take years. During the early days of the CIS it was already clear to me that any breaking of the existing economic ties binding the republics would have meant disaster, not just for Kazakhstan but also for the whole of the Soviet Union. This was why I was so determined that we had to continue working together. There was no point in closing borders which had once been open, nor erecting customs barriers where none had so far existed.

Most crucial of all was the need to retain a single currency, the rouble, across the territory of the entire Commonwealth. Within the European Union, moves were already underway towards the creation of a single currency in place of the existing national currencies of the member states. What was the logic in moving in the opposite direction? Unfortunately, there was a strong current of opinion in Moscow which disagreed.

One of Boris Yeltsin's most important acts in the run-up to the end of the Soviet Union was the choice of his economic team, headed by the young economist Yegor Gaidar, who became his acting Prime Minister. Gaidar and his colleagues had a vision – as much political as economic – to smash the old Communist system and to allow a new market-led system to rise like a phoenix from its ashes. Yet they proved better at destroying than they did at building. They may have been experts on the latest Western economic thought, but knew little about the realities of the Soviet system, about the day-to-day running of its industry and its agriculture. How could they have done? The background of Gaidar and his colleagues was essentially academic. They had not spent any time working in industry and did not understand the psychology of our industrial managers or their needs.

Unfortunately for the other republics – and indeed for Russia itself – Gaidar and his team had no real understanding of the importance of the ties which existed between us. They looked at the statistics and saw that Russia was subsidising the other republics of the Union (although not Kazakhstan), chiefly through the export of Russian oil and other raw materials at prices way below those on the world markets. They became convinced that they should get rid of these subsidies as soon as possible and were prepared to use whatever means they had at their disposal to do so. Unfortunately, they did not realise that the economic costs of breaking the old ties would more than outweigh any benefits from ending the subsidies. Rather than helping Russia at the expense of its neighbours, their policies threatened to drag us all down together.

The first act in the drama began almost immediately after the collapse of the Soviet Union. On 2 January, 1992, Gaidar 'freed' prices. For decades, the people had been used to prices which were fixed by the state. At a stroke, Gaidar swept all the controls away, ushering in a free-for-all which spread panic through the country. Prices quickly began to shoot up.

Kazakhstan could not follow Russia's move immediately – but nor could we ignore it. Our republic has a land border with Russia more than 6,000 kilometres long. As soon as prices began to rise in Russia, it was easy for speculators to cross to northern Kazakhstan, buy up all our goods and resell them for a hefty margin in Russia. The leaders of the Kazakh regions bordering Russia urged us to follow suit. And so we did: beginning on the 2nd, then on the 16th, 24th and 30th of January we gradually 'freed' prices on the different categories of goods. In the meantime, the speculators continued their disruptive work.

Perhaps Gaidar did Kazakhstan and all the other former Soviet republics a favour. The logic of economic reform dictated that, regardless of what Russia did, we would all eventually have had to get rid of price controls. The fact that Russia made the first move, thereby obliging us to follow suit, at least allowed us to deflect some of the criticism at home.

It was already no secret that a substantial section of opinion in Russia wanted to follow this with a currency reform which would have made the rouble a purely Russian currency. But it was some time coming. I decided that if this was to happen, then I wanted to make sure that Kazakhstan was also a part of this rouble zone. There would undoubtedly be a price to pay in terms of some loss of sovereignty: it was clear that the Russians would insist in return on having some control over our budget deficit and money supply. Our central bank would, in effect, become subordinate to the Russian one. However, such a price was worth paying, if it meant that our factories would not lose ties with their traditional business partners and our people's standard of living would not be hit so hard. For this reason, I made clear both to Yeltsin and to his ministers on frequent occasions that if they ever decided to introduce a new currency, they should warn us in advance. They agreed.

Despite such pledges, I was wary of Russia's intentions from the start. For this reason, early in 1992, I issued a secret presidential decree on creating our own national currency and summoned together a group of experts from the finance ministry and the central bank. We met every month behind closed doors to discuss the design and form of the money and to look at possible Western companies which could print it for us.

Everything was done in secret because we did not want to worry our people. Also, we still very much wanted to remain within the rouble zone. The question of money was of more than economic significance; it was also of psychological importance. Whatever the degree of euphoria about independence in 1992, as long as everyone continued to use the same currency, in their hearts people still believed that the Soviet Union continued to exist and that there was some kind of joint roof over our heads. Yet necessarily, the issue was out of our hands: we had to bear in mind the unpredictable nature of the polices being pursued by Russia. We could not allow ourselves to become a hostage of Russian policy.

By the middle of 1992, we had finalised the design and agreed on a British company, Thomas de la Rue, to print the money. When I made the first down payment, I told the company secretly to print a quarter of the total notes required and store them in London so that they would be ready at any moment if we needed them. At the same time, I began secret discussions with the International Monetary Fund and the World Bank on the modalities of introducing the new currency. On my invitation, the IMF also sent a mission to Almaty.

It was a good thing that we were prepared. I still have a lot of friends and former colleagues working in Moscow and, towards the end of 1992, I began to hear rumours that the Russian government was getting ready to introduce its own currency. But when I put the issue to the leadership in Moscow, they denied it. Not entirely convinced, I gave the order to speed up the production of our money.

Gaidar's economic policies had made him unpopular among members of parliament. Although Yeltsin had appointed him as Prime Minister, he had to be confirmed in the post by the Supreme Soviet, and the deputies refused to do this. At a heated session in December, he finally stepped down. Yeltsin nominated in his place Viktor Chernomyrdin, a highly-experienced administrator who had spent much of his career in the gas industry. The Supreme Soviet readily confirmed his position.

Chernomyrdin's first official visit was to Kazakhstan. Within three days of taking office, he came to Almaty. We talked about a number of issues, including the currency question, and we agreed that if Russia did introduce a new rouble, Kazakhstan would remain part of the rouble zone. It was the same story when we met again a few weeks later, at the end of January, at the World Economic Conference in Davos, Switzerland. Some friends organised a dinner, which we both attended with our respective delegations. Afterwards, the two of us went outside to talk alone.

Chernomyrdin told me that the government was planning to introduce some new notes; they would start pulling in the old ones with the portrait of Lenin from 1 April, 1993 and replacing them with new ones.

'Bear in mind, that no one should know,' Chernomyrdin told me. 'But don't worry. We will print money for Kazakhstan as well.'

'All right,' I said. 'But are you sure?'

'Sure,' he said.

'Can I trust you?'

'Yes.'

1 April came and went, and there was no sign of the new notes. May and June followed. Then that July, the Russian National Bank declared that it was putting the new notes into circulation. I immediately called Moscow and asked them to send us our share of the money.

'Everything's been printed, it's all here,' came the reply. 'Your supplies will be there in a week.'

At the beginning of August, I flew to Moscow for talks with Yeltsin and we signed a declaration that Kazakhstan would stay in the rouble zone. But, a week later, our bank notes had still not arrived.

Those few weeks of uncertainty were a disaster both for Kazakhstan and those other republics which had yet to introduce their own currencies. Following the announcement in July, millions of old Soviet roubles which were no longer valid in Russia were being literally dumped in Kazakhstan, severely disrupting the local economy. It was then that I realised that we had to move fast. We prepared to send the planes to London to collect the money.

I met Yeltsin and Chernomyrdin at the beginning of August and then again in the middle of the month. A month passed, and they had still not sent us the promised stock of new roubles. Meanwhile, wagon-loads of old roubles, now worthless in Russia, continued to flood in to Kazakhstan, causing havoc. Our security service established that millions of them were being sent from Chechnya and elsewhere in the Caucasus.

The Russians' intention was clear: they did not know of our secret plans to print our own money and believed that we would accept any conditions that they set us if the alternative was ruin. Initially, at least, we went along with their plan. On 7 October, at a meeting in Moscow, with the representatives of Uzbekistan, Armenia, Tajikistan and Belarus, I signed a framework agreement with the Russians which was to form the basis of a new rouble zone encompassing all six of our republics. The media described it as major step towards creation of an economic union. However, the price which the Russians demanded from us was considerable: we would be allowed to use the new rouble only after unifying our budget, tax, customs and banking policies with those in Russia and giving the Russian central bank control of our money supply. Although it constituted a major loss of sovereignty, I still believed it was in the interest of Kazakhstan, and, when our parliament convened on 12 October, I persuaded them to ratify it. That day, Daulet Sembayev, the first deputy Prime Minister, called Chernomyrdin, who confirmed Russia's intent to introduce the 1993 notes.

But events were moving swiftly in Russia, where the stand-off between Yeltsin and his parliament had culminated in the bloody storming of the White House building just days earlier. A group within the Russian government which opposed the rouble zone agreement was growing in influence.

Just over a week after the ratification vote, Alexander Shokhin, the deputy Russian Prime Minister, came to Almaty. Shokhin, who was a co-chairman of the commission for integrating the monetary systems of the six republics, had ostensibly come to discuss the modalities of the September agreement and the measures which needed to be taken. Once we were behind closed doors, it was clear to me that he had a very different purpose. I asked him directly whether the Russian government was really going to include us in the rouble zone.

'We can't do it,' he said. 'We have already split up. We have separate interests now.'

'So why didn't you tell us this three months ago?' I said.

The meeting broke up without agreement. And, although we agreed to continue our discussions in Moscow the following week, it was clear that the idea was dead. The declarations and joint statements that I had signed with Yeltsin and with Chernomyrdin meant nothing. From the very beginning, they had intended to push Kazakhstan out of the rouble zone. I considered then, and I still consider now, that it was absolutely unjust as far as we were concerned. I had trusted them and believed in our relationship with Russia and they had let us down.

Psychologically, giving up the rouble was an enormous step. Kazakhstan, after all, is an ethnically-mixed state. More than 30 per cent of our people are Russian and still have close ties with Russia; even many Kazakhs have children or parents there. When deciding policy, I had to try to avoid doing anything which would weaken those ties. Introducing a new, separate currency would certainly have that effect. There was also the problem of how we would handle economic ties with Russia which continued to account for a huge slice of Kazakhstan's economy. Despite all this, it was clear after my conversation with Shokhin that we had no alternative but to introduce the tenge. So in mid-October, we sent the transport planes to London to pick up the money.

In retrospect, that was the easy part. When the planes returned, we set ourselves the task of ensuring that the newly printed notes were distributed throughout Kazakhstan. The operation was conducted in complete secrecy under the control of the security ministry. I made clear that anyone who revealed the secret would be fired immediately and taken to court. Within the seemingly impossible period of one week and with incredible energy, they managed to distribute the bank notes across the country to the local authorities, not just to every town and region, but to even the smallest village as well.

In the following weeks speculation grew that we were planning to introduce the tenge, but I said nothing. The value of the old rouble plunged dramatically and inflation went higher, touching an annual rate of over 3,000 per cent. Finally, on 10 November, at a joint press conference, Islam Karimov, the President of neighbouring Uzbekistan, and I announced that we were both abandoning the rouble and each introducing our own currencies in its place. In a joint statement, we said 'The Russian government's conditions for uniting monetary systems are unacceptable and place Uzbekistan and Kazakhstan in an economically disadvantageous position.'

In order to retain an element of surprise, I deliberately did not specify when the new currency would be introduced. Then two days later, on Friday evening, I broke the news in a speech on state television. The tenge would be introduced from the following Monday morning, its value backed by more than 700 million dollars in gold and foreign exchange reserves. Under the terms which I outlined, people would be able to exchange up to 100,000 roubles at a rate of 500 to one tenge. The speed with which we were moving to the new money was not only a surprise for the people of Kazakhstan, who had been oblivious of our secret preparations, but it was also a surprise for the Russian government which could never have expected us to act so quickly.

Our specialists had worked very well and the notes themselves were high quality, but it would be wrong to say that everything went smoothly. As soon as the tenge went into circulation, it became clear that the initial exchange rate of 4.7 to the dollar was far too high. We had no alternative but to devalue it immediately to 20 to the dollar. It was a serious mistake by Sergei Tereshchenko, the Prime Minister, and he should have resigned immediately afterwards, rather than staying on in office, as he did, until October 1994.

The International Monetary Fund estimated that the rate would decline to 150 to the dollar by 1 September, 1994 and 200 by January 1995. In reality, the decline has been much more gradual: the tenge has been floating down by about three to four per cent a month, until by early 1996 it was fairly stable at around 70 to the dollar. Our currency is also now accepted across Central Asia and in Russia. In May 1995, we inaugurated a new British-built plant allowing us to print our own notes and coins. Our monetary independence was complete.

With hindsight, it is clear that, from a purely economic point of view, the Russians acted in their own interests throughout the affair. They could not hope to run a coherent monetary policy if money was being printed in one place but budgets were being decided separately by the governments of the various republics. However, the September agreement should have given them, in principle, all the guarantees that they needed. That is where the deception lay. The Russians should have warned us and the other republics what they were going to do.

This is not necessarily the end of the story. The countries of the European Union have already begun to introduce a single currency, the euro. Why should the former Soviet republics, with their own extensive experience in economic co-operation, not pursue the same aim? The twenty-first century will see an increasing level of international integration. A single currency across the countries of the former Soviet Union could be part of that.

I am often asked what kind of economic system we are trying to build in Kazakhstan. Are we looking towards the developed capitalism of the United States and Britain, or what, until the recent economic crisis in the region, was being described as the Japanese 'miracle' or the so-called 'dragons' of South-East Asia? People are surprised to hear my reply: a Kazakh model.

I remember once seeing an interview on television with Arkady Volsky, the powerful head of Russia's Union of Industrialists and Engineers. The subject was economic reform. One of the journalists asked him what he thought about adopting the 'Swedish model' in Russia, which at the time was considered a great success. 'The model is very good,' he replied, 'but where are we going to get hold of all those Swedes to come and work for us?'

I almost applauded out loud as I watched him. Recent history has shown the folly of adopting wholesale foreign economic models. During the 1970s, Edward Gierek, the Polish Communist leader, was determined to turn his country into one of the world's major economic powers. As a long-time admirer of Japan, he chose to adopt their economic model. Huge amounts of money from the state budget were spent on buying highly sophisticated technology which the experts said would allow the Polish economy to make a great leap forward. Unfortunately, the Japanese economic model did not work on Polish soil. The result was a massive foreign debt. It was only by a series of tough structural reforms in the late 1980s and early 1990s – which had nothing to do with any Japanese model – that the Polish economy was at last able to recover.

Kazakhstan has long since outgrown the childish notion that there is some kind of an ideal, universal model which can simply be applied to our own country. Such models do not exist. Kazakhstan has its own specifics, its own traditions and a population with its own particular mentality. We must create our own system, which will be based on the general principles of market economics.

Our aim is to form a social market economy, based on competitive principles, with a combination and interaction of the main forms of ownership, both private and state, each of which will perform its own functions in the overall system of economic and social inter-relationships. In Kazakhstan, there will be no liberal or 'popular' capitalism, no 'true' or 'modernised' socialism, but simply a normal democratic society with a multi-tiered market economy that opens up equal opportunities for independent choice and economic self-determination in the pursuit of everyone's economic, social, national and political interests.

A flourishing society can be reached only through the market and through an open economy. But there must also be comprehensive support for its enterprises. This is the only way of achieving the transformation of the economy which is the cornerstone of our conceptual model of the country's development. It is a difficult task.

For this reason, during my annual speech to the people of Kazakhstan in October 1996, I warned them that their living standards and social services, maybe even the survival of the state itself, depended on the state of the economy and the degree to which it was reformed.

Kazakhstan is still going through a complex economic crisis which is the result of the decades during which it was run under the Communist system of central planning; this had already exhausted its potential by the beginning of the 1970s. Unfortunately, we will continue to feel the effects of this system for many years to come; not just until we have changed the whole basis of the economy but until the mentality of the population has been transformed as well. The problem has been enhanced both by the Kazakh economy's dependence on raw materials and by the closeness with which it is integrated with the economies of the other republics of the former Soviet Union. The break-up of the Union and its replacement by a number of separate enclaves forced us to look again at the traditional markets in which we used to buy and sell our goods. This, in turn, led to a dramatic fall in production.

The attempts to co-ordinate financial and credit policy in a single rouble zone proved impossible. The egoism of the various republics and the uncontrolled emission of money fuelled an inflationary spiral. Government revenues were sharply hit by the decline in production and the end to traditional forms of financing, which, in turn, had a serious adverse affect on spending both on investment and in the social sphere, leading to a plunge in people's living standards.

The mishandling of the exchange rate of the tenge was not the only mistake made by Tereshchenko. His government made other errors in economic policy, leading to the cabinet resigning in its entirety in 1994. It was replaced by a new cabinet of ministers under Akezhan Kazhegeldin, which began to carry out reform more dynamically and effectively. Slowly, the situation began to improve.

Already, by the beginning of 1996, thanks to the speeding up of the reform process and to the help which Kazakhstan was receiving from international economic organisations, we were able to stabilise the macro-economy. This allowed us to ensure that economic activity flowed into more logical and controllable channels.

Annual inflation, which had stood at more than 2,400 per cent in 1993, fell to just 60 per cent by 1995. In 1996, it was around 30 per cent and was expected to fall much further, to around 10 per cent, by the end of 1998. A sharp cut in government spending also allowed us to keep the budget in 1996 to within the limits set by the International Monetary Fund of 3.3 per cent of GDP. For the first time in seven years, production stopped falling and actually began to grow a little; the range of goods which we are able to export is also expanding. Scenes typical of the period before 1991, when huge lines used to form outside every shop which had anything to sell, have receded into history. People now have a genuine choice when it comes to buying goods.

Another important achievement has been privatisation. This is extremely significant for a country such as Kazakhstan, whose economy has been dominated since earliest times by the state sector. The process of privatisation began slowly in 1993, when we auctioned 14 shops in Almaty, raising the equivalent of US$322,000. A similar process was then extended across the country, including trading companies, food suppliers and other service providers. Parallel to this, we began mass-privatisation of apartments, which allowed us to create a properly functioning housing market in a short space of time. We then moved to the second phase, involving the sale into the private sector of large state enterprises.

Some major foreign companies quickly became involved. One of the first was Philip Morris, the US tobacco and food conglomerate. In December 1993, the company took a 97 per cent stake in the Almaty Tobacco Factory in return for investing a total of US $315 million. Their aim was to increase annual production of cigarettes from 16 billion to 25 billion. It has been described as one of the most successful privatisations in the entire CIS. Other early successes included the Almaty and Karaganda Margarine Combines and the Shymkent Confectionery Factory.

By 1996, privatised companies made up around 80 per cent of the economy: in the agricultural sector, private firms and other new forms of property ownership accounted for 97 per cent; in industry, 80 per cent; in construction, 82 per cent and in transport, 48 per cent. As far as the total national product was concerned, the private sector accounted for some 55–60 per cent (in agriculture, the figure was 90 per cent, in construction, 60 per cent and in trade, 80 per cent). We can honestly say that the private sector is now established throughout the economy and, in virtually every sector except for industry, transport and telecommunications, it is already the dominant force.

We have paid great attention to the development and modernisation of the transport sector and of telecommunications. One of the main achievements has been the completion of the Transasian railway which links the Pacific Ocean coast with the Bosphorus. We and our trading partners now have the possibility of direct access both to the ports of the Pacific and to those of the Persian Gulf and the Mediterranean. We have also begun to build a modern international airport near Almaty for passengers and freight as well as a new oil pipeline running from east to west. All this will speed up the integration of Kazakhstan into the world economy, helping to turn it into a bridge between East and West, between the countries of Europe and the Turkic and Pacific nations.

Despite the difficult economic situation, we also made considerable efforts to try to raise people's living standards and to improve their social protection. Particular emphasis has been put on the situation of the poorest members of society. In all, average salaries over the last two years increased by a factor of 3.9. Further proof of the improvement came from statistics showing that deposits at commercial banks rose by a factor of 5.6.

However clear the turning point in the economic situation, it would be wrong to say that we have succeeded in solving all our problems. Unfortunately, much still remains to be done: in a short space of time we must complete the reform of enterprises and the basic sectors of the economy, conclude the privatisation process, carry out a reform of the financial and banking sector, improve the situation with state revenue and the way that it is spent and, finally, solve the problem of non-payment of bills. None of this is easy. However, we have already proved how much we can achieve, given our determination.

Foreign investment has been vital. More than US$2 billion has already been invested in Kazakhstan, primarily in the oil, gas and mining sectors which are of great interest to foreign investors. There is also huge potential for further foreign investment in the metal and chemical industries, as well as in energy, telecommunications and manufacturing. Five years ago, there were only about a dozen US companies active in Kazakhstan; today there are around 100, as well as another 900 from other Western countries. They include more than 50 oil companies, which have already invested heavily in joint ventures exploiting the hydrocarbon resources.

The improving situation has been widely noted. A recent report by the World Bank pointed to increasing flows of direct foreign investment and joint ventures and praised the government's increasing market-oriented liberalisation: 'Kazakhstan's long-term economic prospects are excellent, given its vast hydrocarbon and mineral resources, low external debt obligations and well-trained work force.'

We have already achieved much towards giving Kazakhstan a dynamic, developing market economy, but there is more to be done. As Ludwig Erhard, the post-war West German Chancellor who presided over that country's *Wirtschaftswunder*, put it, we have to go through the purgatory of reforms not just for the sake of reforms themselves but so that we can emerge as a new nation. We are still feeling the burden of the past, both economically and psychologically, but the path for the future has been laid down and we can say confidently that all the prerequisites are there: not just huge natural resources, but also industrial and agricultural sectors with considerable export potential as well as progressive legislation, higher education and a good skill base among the population. It is not by mere chance that, of all the CIS and former Eastern bloc countries, it is Kazakhstan that is set to obtain the largest share of investments over the next ten years. According to a United Nations study, we should attract 47 billion dollars out of a total US$103 billion of foreign investment committed to the former Communist countries, putting us well ahead of Russia. This means that investors trust us and believe in Kazakhstan. It is a trust which we will not betray.

CHAPTER EIGHT

THE ETHNIC MOSAIC

THE ethnic riots of December 1986 showed the fragility of ethnic relations within Kazakhstan and the disastrous consequences of handling them wrongly. Providing a framework within which Kazakhs, Russians, Ukrainians, Germans, Koreans and the many other nationalities of Kazakhstan can live peacefully together is one of the main challenges which we face today. But it is one which we want to solve on our own, without interference by outsiders.

For the first time in its modern history, Kazakhstan has the opportunity to revive the traditions not just of the Kazakhs themselves, but also of all the nationalities which make up the diverse mosaic of the republic's population: national consensus is thus a fundamental premise of domestic policy. Due to the complicated ethnic composition of our state, it is vital that we ensure the principle of equal opportunity and equality before the law for everyone, regardless of their national affiliation.

The entire history of the Soviet Union, beginning with the revolution in 1917, is a history of the violation of human rights and even of genocide, which has pushed not just the Kazakhs but also many of the other non-Russian nations to the edge of disaster: the famine of the 1920s and 1930s caused by the enforced collectivisation of agriculture claimed the lives of millions of people; the shooting or imprisonment in labour camps by Stalin of millions more innocent people and the deportation, largely to Kazakhstan, of entire nations who fell out of favour with the authorities were among the most dramatic examples.

Among such infringements of human rights, I would include the creation of the million-strong armies of workers who were deployed to build massive industrial complexes, railways, canals and various military test ranges. Many of these people, known in the official propaganda of the time as 'enthusiasts', ended up in Kazakhstan. I remember Boris Oleynik, a celebrated Ukrainian poet, describing, during one of the last Communist Party conferences, how things happened during the Soviet years. 'It was decided to build, for example, a power station in Ukraine,' he said bitterly. 'And what about the native peoples? Like the native Indians of America, they were made to leave their homes and flee the "conquerors". And this was happening in the twentieth century.'

To understand the current ethnic situation in Kazakhstan, it is necessary to go back further still, to Tsarist times. During the nineteenth century, there was already mass-emigration from Russia, Ukraine and Belarus to what were considered the 'empty' lands of Kazakhstan. This continuous stream grew in intensity during the first decade of this century when Pyotr Stolypin implemented his agricultural reform. Every year, some 140,000 people streamed into the republic. Around one fifth of the new arrivals, unable to adapt to the different and often harsh conditions of life, returned home to the European part of the Soviet Union, but the remainder, some 1.2 million of them, settled in Kazakhstan for good. For that reason, my opinion of Stolypin has always differed from that of modern-day Russian historians. However much he did to advance reform, he made a number of mistakes in his policy and, by encouraging this mass-migration, caused the Kazakh people considerable suffering.

Later, during the collectivisation of the late 1920s and early 1930s, some 250,000 so-called *kulaks*, peasants whose only crime was to be a little wealthier than the broad mass of their fellow countrymen, were stripped of their property and sent to Kazakhstan. Also during these years, almost the entire territory of the republic was turned into a place of exile for hundreds of thousands of opponents of the Communist system, most of whom were completely innocent of any crime, as well as many genuine criminals. A network of prisons, camps and exile settlements was built across Kazakhstan to accommodate them. Even when their sentences finished, many Russian-speaking prisoners were not allowed to return to their home cities in Russia and stayed behind. Another 1.2 million people were sent from Russia, Ukraine, Belarus, the Baltic States and Moldova to work in factories in Kazakhstan during this pre-war period.

A decade later, after the outbreak of World War II, whole nations were deported and dumped in Kazakhstan, chiefly the Volga Germans, Crimean Tartars, Chechens and Ingush. Accused *en masse* of traitorous sentiments and anti-Soviet activity, the people – predominantly the elderly, women and children – were suddenly rounded up and loaded on to cattle trucks, without even being given time to collect their belongings together, and sent on the horrific two-week journey eastwards. Tens of thousands of them died of hunger, cold or disease as they crossed the steppes. The figures show the enormity of what happened: some 18,500 Korean families were deported from the Far East, as well as 800,000 Germans from the Volga, 102,000 Poles from the west of the Soviet Union and 507,000 Chechens and other indigenous people from the North Caucasus. Many of those born in exile went on to be leading political figures in the Soviet Union – among them Dzhokar Dudayev, the first President of Chechnya, and Ruslan Khasbulatov, who served as speaker of the Russian parliament.

According to official figures, the population of Kazakhstan increased by more than one and a half million as a result of these movements of people. The true figure was probably considerably higher. During the war, another 350,000 people were evacuated to Kazakhstan, along with factories which were moved south-eastwards out of the way of the advancing German army. Many members of the Soviet cultural and scientific élite also came here.

Such mass-immigration continued in the years after the war and, although it was largely voluntary, its effects on Kazakhstan were often negative. Under Nikita Khrushchev's so-called 'Virgin Lands' programme of the 1950s and 1960s, some two and a half million people came, largely from the European parts of the Soviet Union, to settle in the north of Kazakhstan. They were joined by another 150,000 or so who came to work in military plants. As the name suggests, official Soviet propaganda maintained that these lands were somehow empty and abandoned. In fact, Kazakh herders lived there, dividing up the territory between themselves according to a centuries-old tradition. They knew how to take care of the land too, constantly varying their pasture areas in order to avoid the soil becoming depleted. No one in Moscow asked the permission of these local people before they sent in the settlers. As a result, the Soviet Union as a whole lost an important source of livestock. Indeed, the economic results would have been much better if Khrushchev had taken the same amount of money which he spent on Kazakhstan and invested it in agriculture within Russia instead. However, as so often in the Soviet period, the policy was dictated by political considerations rather than common sense.

Throughout these years, though, there was a process of what one could call natural migration – namely, intelligent and ambitious people who came to Kazakhstan in order to turn their good ideas into reality. Although they brought with them their own national cultures and traditions, many of these people were especially open to the Kazakh way of life. They form a good example for our future trading partners: to be successful in Kazakhstan it is wise to respect the country's traditions and culture.

For the Kazakhs, the low-point came in the 1960s. At the end of the last century they had still accounted for some 90 per cent of the population of Kazakhstan; just over half a century later this had plummeted to 29 per cent, a smaller proportion than the indigenous population of any other Soviet republic. The republic was still named after them – but they were a minority within it. The situation began to improve slightly thereafter, and their share of the population has since crept back up to 50 per cent.

In reality, the nationalities policy of the Soviet Union – or rather of the Soviet Communist Party – was a continuation of that pursued by the Russian empire. However strident the ideological slogans and the lip service that was paid to the national self-determination of peoples, in reality Lenin and his successors behaved much as the Tsars had done. The interests of those peoples who lived in the far-flung parts of the country were largely ignored: if they dared to rebel, then they were brutally put down. At the same time, their national traditions and languages were wiped out.

I remember a speech by Leonid Brezhnev, the former Soviet leader, in which he described how the various peoples of the Soviet Union shone like the edges of diamonds, each with their own colour, language and culture. As was the fashion in those days, this simile was then repeated over and over again in the speeches of local leaders. Yet everything was done to ensure that the Kazakhs forgot their great history, traditions, customs and language. The reality was that Kazakhs were deliberately being

Fig. 18 Astana, the new capital of Kazakhstan.

FIG. 19 On an official visit to the Islamic Republic of Iran. With Ali Akbar Hashemi Rafsanjani. Tehran, May 1996.

FIG. 20 With President Jacques Chirac, Paris, June 1995.

FIG. 21 The first official visit to Kazakhstan of the leader of China, Tsiang Tse-Min.
Almaty, July 1996.

FIG. 22 With HRH Prince Charles, the Prince of Wales.
Almaty, November 1996.

FIG. 23 On a visit to the agricultural region, 1996

FIG. 24 With Chancellor Helmut Kohl, The Federal Chancellor of Germany. Bonn, May 1997.

FIG. 25 Talks in Almaty to resolve the inter-ethnic conflict in Tajikistan, May 1995

turned into second-class citizens within their own republic and this could not but make them resentful.

I will never get over the determination of the Soviet historians to fit everything into an ideological straitjacket which led them to turn even the most distant history upside-down. The struggle which Kenisari Quasim-Uli and his forces waged against the Tsarist colonisers during the 1830s and 1840s was presented as a purely nationalistic, feudal movement against the interests of the people. Others of our national heroes were simply written out of history. Nothing was said about the colonisation of Kazakhstan – which was particularly intense during the nineteenth century. Collectivisation was presented as a great service to the people: the inculcation of the idea of proletarian revolution among the nomadic and steppe-land Kazakhs. Only historians *outside* the Soviet Union discussed the real consequences: how hundreds of thousands of people died after their only means of existence, their livestock, was taken away from them; and how the Stalinist purges almost completely wiped out the native Kazakh intelligentsia.

In his book *Snowstorm Halt*, based on real experience of life on the Kazakh steppes, Chingiz Aitmatov, the well-known Kyrgyz writer, has a character, Mankurt, who has been forcibly deprived of the memory of his roots and of the history of his home-land. He is condemned to degenerate and die, because the earth cannot tolerate a person who is not part of the system of historical ties and of nature. By destroying the spiritual life of the people, the Soviet system tried to turn us all into people like Mankurt. How else could one explain the determination of the Bolsheviks to elimi-nate all national differences, a process which they graced with the term 'the coming together of nations'.

At the centre of this was the attempt to eliminate the Kazakh language: this was shown by the text of the various constitutions. While the first constitution of the Soviet period – strictly speaking that of the Kyrgyz (Kazakh) Autonomous Republic – recognised both Kazakh and Russian as national languages, the Kazakh constitutions adopted in 1937 and 1977 spoke only of Russian. In this way the legal basis was created for the total Russification of the Kazakhs.

An especially damaging part of this was the decision, taken under Stalin, to replace the Arabic alphabet traditionally used to write the Kazakh language, first, with the Latin alphabet and then, a few years later, with the Cyrillic one. Even in pre-Revolu-tionary Kazakhstan, where illiteracy prevailed, there had always been two or three people in each community who could read and write. Written history and a wealth of literature had developed over centuries. With these two changes of alphabet, in rapid succession, Stalin not only created enormous confusion among the people, he also succeeded in breaking the link between the new generations and their history. What other explanation could there be for such a move? Many important works were lost in the process and only now are our scientists beginning to repair the damage.

Parallel with the reduction of the Kazakh's share of the population came the decline in their native language. Gradually Kazakh schools were closed and replaced by Russian ones. Many Kazakhs did not want their children to bother to learn Kazakh, because they did not think that it had any future. By then, all further education in Kazakhstan was being conducted exclusively in Russian. 'If you want your children to get on in life, then forget about your native language and send your children to a Russian school,' was a common motto among parents during the 1950s and 1960s. Such a philosophy was not confined to northern Kazakhstan, where the concentration of immigrants was highest. Even in parts of the republic where 90–95 per cent of the population was still Kazakh, Russian became the preferred language of communication. The Kazakh intelligentsia, especially writers, poets and playwrights, began losing ground. It hardly made sense to publish literature in Kazakh any more because the potential readership was declining so rapidly. Anyone who spoke out in defence of their own language and culture was in danger of being accused of nationalism.

The same fate befell other languages. The official line was to point out, at every possible opportunity, the long list of languages in which newspapers, magazines and books were published in Kazakhstan. What actually happened defied all logic: most of the journalists working for, say, the Korean-language newspaper, *Lenin Kichi – Lenin's Flag* – did not even know Korean; they wrote their articles in Russian and had to have them translated. Nor could they find many Koreans who were able to read them. In a desperate attempt to drum up circulation, they used to travel around the areas where the Koreans lived, telling them it was their national duty to subscribe. In the end, the newspapers just gave in and published articles in both Korean and Russian alongside one another. The same thing happened with the *Deutsche Allgemeine Zeitung,* the German-language newspaper.

The decline in the Kazakh language and culture was an important factor in triggering the unrest of December 1986. However, far from learning from what happened, the Soviet authorities did exactly the opposite. By blaming the events on Kazakh nationalism and increasing their heavy-handed attempts to impose 'internationalism' they only added to the tension and made things worse.

Even when the authorities did belatedly intervene on behalf of the Kazakh language, it was half-hearted and badly organised. Having done its best to wipe out Kazakh, the Communist Party then decided to launch a mass campaign to make everyone learn it. However, in a typically ridiculous touch, they failed to provide any books or dictionaries, and there were few qualified teachers. It was decided to re-open some Kazakh schools or at least to organise Kazakh classes in some Russian ones. This often verged on the absurd. I remember the case of one school in Almaty which they decided to divide into two parts: one Kazakh and one Russian. There were two head teachers, two teaching staffs and two separate zones in the same school; the two parts were separated from each other by a high metal fence. The whole town was unhappy with this and one day the pupils just tore the fence down. It made me wonder how many fences they would have had to put up in the little school which I went to in Chemolgan, not just to separate the Kazakhs and the Russians, but also the Ukrainians, Germans, Chechens, Ingush, Koreans and all the others.

As well as language, there were other pressing inter-ethnic problems which had to be solved: one was the restoration of justice to those peoples who had been forcibly deported to Kazakhstan. In the mid-1950s, during the period of the so-called Khruschev thaw, members of the Chechen minority asked to be allowed to return to their homeland in the North Caucasus. Formally, their request was granted. However, as ever, the plans were not worked out properly. When the Chechens arrived back in their homeland they found that no one was expecting them. Worse, most of their houses had long since been occupied by other people. This often led to bloodshed. Despairing of ever receiving justice, many of the Chechens had little alternative but to return to Kazakhstan.

At the end of the 1980s, the question of rehabilitating the other deported peoples and allowing them to return to their homeland arose again. I felt strongly for them and tried on several occasions to press their case with the Soviet leadership. I thought the authorities should not only rehabilitate these people, but also make them a formal apology. I never received any real support from Moscow.. It was all little more than empty declarations.

In particular, this affected the Crimean Tartars, a large number of whom continue to live in Kazakhstan and in the Central Asian republics to this day. After the Tartars demanded to be allowed to return to Crimea, in the Ukraine, from where they had been deported, the authorities in Moscow gave the corresponding order to the Ukrainian authorities. The Ukrainians claimed that they were not against the idea, but asked the Central Committee of the Communist Party to introduce a rule whereby the republics where such deported people had been living in the meantime were obliged to pay compensation to their homeland in order to help cover the cost of building them homes and giving them work. The Central Committee genuinely tried to persuade us to agree, but I was categorically opposed: why should Kazakhstan, which had been given no choice as to whether it wanted to take in these people in the first place, pay compensation decades later? Why should we be forced to assume material, if not moral responsibility, for Stalin's crimes?

The problem was one for the Soviet authorities in Moscow to solve. Although we were not against providing some help to these people for purely humanitarian reasons, we did not want to set a dangerous precedent: there were hundreds of thousands of Germans, Turks, Chechens and other groups living in Kazakhstan who might demand similar treatment. In the end, nothing happened and only small groups of Crimean Tartars returned to Ukraine, largely at their own expense.

In some cases, I tried to solve the problem myself. One such instance concerned the Meskhetian Turks, a small national group who had been deported to Kazakhstan during the war from a region of Georgia, bordering Turkey. On their request, I wrote to the Georgian government asking for help to allow the return of several hundred of these Meskhetian Turk families to their homeland. The reply came back quickly: the Georgians were prepared to allow back some of them, but not more than a few dozen families. When I met the leaders of the Meskhetian Turk community and passed on the message, they were deeply offended. Thanking me for my support, their elders said that they would prefer to stay in Kazakhstan instead.

Even more sensitive was the question of the fate of the ethnic Germans who had been deported to Kazakhstan when their own republic on the banks of the River Volga was dissolved during the war and absorbed into the Russian region of Saratov. They were divided as to what they actually wanted: one group was pressing hard for the restoration of the former German Volga republic, while a second group, believing this to be impossible, wanted my help in making it easier for them to emigrate to Germany. Then there was a third, more realistic, group which wanted Kazakhstan to do more to help revive their traditions, language and culture and to establish better relations between their community and with Germany itself.

Although it was this third approach which appealed most to me, I tried to examine all the possibilities during meetings with the Russian and German governments on this problem. Despite the difficulty of the situation, I am convinced that we are making some progress, even if it is not as fast as I would like.

One of the reasons why ethnic tensions have continued in Kazakhstan is the way that the damaging nationalities policies, which were carried out during the Soviet period, were associated in the minds of many Kazakhs with the Russians. This is not surprising. These attempts to unify the way of life, traditions and culture of the peoples of the Soviet Union, to create a truly 'Soviet people', were carried out in a Russian form and in the Russian language. This attempt at forced assimilation could not fail to antagonise the Kazakhs, and indeed virtually all the other non-Russian peoples of the Soviet Union. Even within the core Slavic republics of Ukraine and Belarus, anti-Russian feeling was strong and has continued to this day. After Kazakhstan gained independence in 1991, a substantial proportion of the Kazakh people felt a kind of euphoria that we had somehow scored a victory over the Russians. Such sentiments certainly did not help inter-ethnic relations. However, I am pleased to say that the majority of Kazakhs behaved in a calm, sensible and pragmatic way, adhering to our centuries-old tradition of living in peace with our neighbours.

For myself and my colleagues, one of our most important tasks has been to maintain stability and to overcome the sudden cooling in inter-ethnic relations, which could become a very serious problem. We have tried to find, as quickly as possible, a way of creating a feeling of solidarity between the various national groups in our society. My election as President and the results of the referendum on extending my term of office helped this process. The fact that I was supported by a clear majority of people from all the ethnic groups added to my confidence that we will be able to avoid any kind of inter-ethnic cataclysm. Our goal of achieving inter-ethnic consensus means more than just improving relations between Kazakhs and Russians: we must also ensure that the Ukrainians, Germans, Koreans and all the other groups living in Kazakhstan feel themselves to be united, with equal rights and equal feelings of patriotism.

A major part in all this must be played by the Kazakh people. For the first time in modern history, independence has given the Kazakhs the chance to assume a leading role in our country; it has given them a real possibility to rule their state, to transform the economy and revive the national culture, traditions and language. Only the Kazakhs can, and should, assume responsibility for the fate of the multi-ethnic population of Kazakhstan, helping people from other national groups to adapt to the new circumstances, creating together an atmosphere free from any attempts to destabilise society and encouraging unity. After living for two centuries under Tsarist domination, and then for seven decades under the Soviets, the Kazakhs as a nation are uniquely placed to guarantee that no individual national group will ever be oppressed again.

The Kazakhs have a long tradition of supporting peace and living alongside other nations and peoples. They are also tolerant, patient, and well-meaning, and respect the way of life, customs and cultures of others. Their good qualities were summed up by Khodzha Akhmet Yassaui, a Sufi poet, who is considered by Muslims to be second only to the holy Mohammed:

> The prophet has this wish:
> When one day you meet a stranger,
> Do not do him wrong.
> God does not love people with cruel hearts.

These words are written on his mausoleum in the town of Turkestan, in Kazakhstan, which is considered by Muslims as a little Mecca and is a place of pilgrimage for believers from across the Islamic world. The Kazakh people are always true to the words of their prophets.

The equal rights of the different national groups living in Kazakhstan have been further strengthened by the constitutional reforms which were carried out in 1995. The old Soviet-era constitution described Kazakhstan as a republic in which the Kazakhs would achieve self-determination. The current document is much fairer. It begins with the words: 'We, the people of Kazakhstan …'. There is no suggestion that this is a state for Kazakhs only. Instead, it is written that Kazakhstan is a country with a multi-ethnic citizenry, and one which defends the rights of all citizens, regardless of their nationality, religious faith, political conviction and so on. In which other country, including the Slavic ones of the former Soviet Union, has the question of inter-ethnic relations been settled in such a way?

We have reached the same compromise as far as language is concerned: under the current constitution, the status of Kazakh has been strengthened as the state language, while Russian has become the official language, used on an equal basis in all organisations and institutions. By doing this, we have managed to remove the tension from what was, until recently, one of the most divisive issues which we faced. I believe that while both Kazakh and Russian should be state languages, it would be even better to give some other, although lesser, status to English as well. Unfortunately, however, society is not yet ready for this.

To achieve equality between the languages, we must also take measures to help arrest the decline into which Kazakh has gone over the years. This means encouraging its use in the civil service, in industry, science and education so that it becomes as widespread as Russian. At the moment, Russian still predominates in many sectors of life, especially at work, and even in the legal system. As long as a substantial proportion of the people working in the legal system, not to mention the policemen themselves, do not know Kazakh, then legal proceedings will have to be conducted in Russian. Fortunately, the people of Kazakhstan appreciate this.

Helping the Kazakh language does not mean that we are trying to drive out the Russian language or Russian-speakers from various spheres of activity, as some of our opponents try to claim: many Russian-speakers are, in fact, ethnic Kazakhs who do not know their native language. On the contrary, we are doing as much as we can to create the right conditions for all people in this country, and especially the Kazakhs, to learn the Kazakh language. Certainly there will be some jobs, especially in the civil service and the government, which will be open only to people who speak Kazakh, but there is nothing nationalist about this. Take the post of President. Anyone wanting to stand for this post must be able to speak Kazakh, but this does not prevent the candidature of a Russian, for example, or a Korean or German, provided that he has learnt enough of the language to carry out his official duties.

Anyone who accuses us of discriminating against Russian-speakers should study the facts: our government meetings are conducted in Russian, as are the sessions of our parliament; parents who want to educate their children in Russian are free to do so, more than half the schools in the country are Russian-language ones, more than enough to meet the requirements of the Russian-speaking population; newspapers are printed in seven different languages; theatres work in six; radio and television are broadcast not just in Kazakh and Russian but also in minority languages such as German, Uygur and Korean; there are more than 300 publications in different languages, of which 70 per cent are in Russian. In Kazakhstan it is also expressly forbidden to infringe anyone's rights on grounds of lack of knowledge of the state language or of any other language, or on grounds of nationality, faith, party affiliation and so on.

The Kazakhs themselves have no interest in suppressing the Russian language: if anything, we need it even more than the Russians do. Knowledge of Russian has always given us access not just to Russian culture but also to the world of science and technology. Russian is a world language and one of the official languages of the United Nations. We have to respect that. On a personal level, the ties are even stronger. If you look today at the intellectual potential of our country, then it is the generation of 30 to 35 year olds with degrees from universities and institutes in Moscow and St Petersburg. In which language did they study? Russian. My own example is a good illustration: I was educated in Russian and brought up with both Kazakh and Russian culture. Even today, I still count Russians among my friends. By profession, I am a metallurgist, but this is not a skill which is native to Kazakhstan. I was taught by experts from the Russian metalworks of the Urals. For that reason, the expression 'internationalism', although derided by some as a relic of Soviet days, has always been a reality for me.

In 1995, we marked the 150th anniversary of the birth of Abai, the great Kazakh poet, philosopher and teacher. He left behind the enormous treasure of his writings, most notable among them a collection of advice on how the good man should live his life. I remember especially one passage from this: 'The knowledge of the language and culture of another nation makes a man equal with these people, he feels himself free. And if their hopes and worries are close to his heart, then he can never stand aside from them.'

The Russians have reacted to the changes brought about by independence in a very different way from the Kazakhs. With the break-up of the Soviet Union, they were turned overnight from 'first among equals' to 'equal among equals'. This was very difficult for many of them, especially for those who had not established very deep roots in this country. Many of these Russians, as well as some Ukrainians, Germans and members of other minority groups, have left Kazakhstan over the past few years. Some have criticised the government for this, as if we were to blame, implying that we have somehow driven them out. This is not true. After long analysis of the situation, I have come to the conclusion that many of the people who left were suffering from a kind of psychological stress. Those brought up in the Soviet Union had got used to living within what was essentially a unitary state where it was largely irrelevant in which republic you lived. In 1991 this changed, literally overnight. Many of the non-native peoples of the various republics, including Kazakhstan, suddenly felt themselves to be living abroad, cut off from their homeland and abandoned to their fate. As border guards and customs posts began to appear along the frontiers – something, incidentally, to which Kazakhstan was opposed – and citizenship laws were passed, many people panicked and hurried back to their homeland, in the fear that one day return might no longer be possible. The process was exacerbated by the economic and political chaos and uncertainty which were a feature of the early 1990s. Many people were afraid and wanted to go back to their historical roots, to be with their families. However regrettable, there was something inevitable about it as the Soviet Union split up into its constituent parts.

This process should not be over-dramatised. Most of those who left were not those whose families had lived here for two or three generations, but rather the more recent arrivals: those who were deported to Kazakhstan in the 1930s, for example, those who arrived during the war when factories were evacuated here and those who came as Young Communists to work on 'opening up' the Virgin Lands or else to build factories or military test ranges. Many had always intended returning home after a few years, or, at the latest, when they reached retirement age.

Unfortunately for Kazakhstan, those who left included some of the most hard-working and the most skilled, who could have made a vital contribution to solving our economic problems. It is not our job to prevent them from going, but neither are we passively watching all this happening. Since independence, the government has de-voted a lot of attention to the issue of migration and to the implementation of effective demographic policies. For example, we concluded an agreement with Russia making it easier to grant citizenship to Kazakhs working permanently in Russia and to Russians who want to come to work in our country. This is more fundamental than merely regulating the process of immigration and emigration; it should also help to remove the concerns of those Russian speakers who were living in Kazakhstan and who had returned to Russia because they feared that they might not be allowed to do so in the future. The government is also considering other measures aimed at encouraging all non-Kazakhs currently living here to stay. Some of the Kazakh nationalist groups have sharply criticised me for this policy, but I am convinced that it is in the best interests of the whole country.

Whenever the subject of Russian emigration is brought up, I am reminded of a conversation which I had with Shimon Peres, the former Israeli Prime Minister. He told me that 700,000 Jews had emigrated from Russia to Israel over the last few years. Others leave Russia for the West. But does anyone in these countries blame the Russian government for that? People should be free to live where they choose. And, in any case, whose fault is it that so many million Russians ended up outside the borders of Russia? It is certainly not the fault of the Kazakhs nor of the indigenous population of the other former Soviet republics to which they have migrated.

Some Russian politicians, keen to play the 'nationalist card', have often brought up the question of these 20 million ethnic Russians who live in the other former Soviet republics, claiming that they are being mistreated and urging the Russian government to intervene on their behalf. Such statements, often made by mainstream figures, merely serve to inflame passions within the countries where they live and have an adverse affect on international relations. I have complained about this to the Russian leadership.

Ultimately, the problem is not with Kazakhstan and the other republics, but with Russia itself which has yet to work out a coherent policy towards its Diaspora. Some in Russia call for all these people to return to their homeland in order to help to rebuild it. However, they do not address the question of where they will find the money needed to build homes and provide work for these people. Imagine the crisis if all these *emigré* Russians suddenly turned up in Russia, with nowhere to live and no work. Other, equally irresponsible people, most notably Vladimir Zhirinovsky, the now largely discredited right-wing Russian politician (who, by unfortunate coincidence, was born in Almaty), simply demand the restoration of the Russian empire within its own borders, or else the annexing of territories close to the border. Russian nationalists, many of them Cossacks from the other side of the border, have also tried to foment tension in what they wrongly consider to be the Russian lands of northern Kazakhstan. This is simply playing with fire.

As far as the Cossacks are concerned, I have stressed on a number of occasions that I will do nothing to stop their attempts to revive their history and culture and form communities in which they live and work together. On the contrary, I will encourage it. This tolerance ends if they start carrying weapons or forming armed organisations, both of which are expressly forbidden by law. There can be no exception for them, regardless of their militaristic history. If they want to bear arms, then let them serve in the Kazakh army as regular soldiers and officers. There can be no separate Cossack regiments which are subordinated to Atamans rather than the regular chain of command. If the Russians object to this, then I would put the following question to them; would the Russian government allow on its territory special military units which took their orders from, say, China? If not, then why should such illegal formations be allowed in Kazakhstan? That being said, relations between the Kazakh authorities and the leaders of the Cossack community are good. We meet on many occasions and often succeed in finding a common approach to our problems.

I remember, with regret, the intervention which Alexander Solzhenitsyn, the celebrated writer and Nobel laureate, made in 1990. From his exile in Vermont, Solzhenitsyn wrote a pamphlet in which he demanded, among other things, the separation of the north of Kazakhstan from the rest of the country and its addition to Russia, Ukraine and Belarus to form a Slavic union. When news of his views reached Kazakhstan it virtually caused a riot. The crisis passed but it is a shame that a man as great as Solzhenitsyn, who actually spent many years in Kazakhstan during his time in the camps, should understand so little of the reality of the situation.

It is important to note that since the mid-1990s, the number of ethnic Russians leaving Kazakhstan has been steadily decreasing. The number of ethnic Germans leaving is also stabilising. People have begun to think more carefully before making such a dramatic move. If they do decide to leave, then it tends to be for much more concrete reasons; whether to go back to elderly relatives, to start families or because they have been offered a better-paid job elsewhere.

One of the most painful legacies of the Soviet period with which we are now having to contend concerns those Kazakhs who were forced to flee abroad. Some five million Kazakhs currently live outside Kazakhstan, around half of them beyond the borders of the former Soviet Union. They left Kazakhstan at different times and for different reasons: some fled during the Tsarist years, others after the 1917 revolution and the civil war which followed. The largest exodus, though, occurred at the beginning of the 1930s following the start of forced collectivisation. From 1931 to 1933 more than one and half million Kazakhs and another half a million people of other nationalities died from the famine which was deliberately started by the authorities. The whole gene fund of the nation was under threat. This, in turn, provoked a huge outflow of people: to the region around the Volga, to the North and Transcaucasus, to Central Asia and to the central regions of Russia, to the Urals, Siberia and the Altai. Hundreds of thousands of Kazakhs left the territory of the Soviet Union completely, fleeing to Mongolia, China, Afghanistan, Iran, Turkey and other countries.

Many of them dreamed of returning to their homeland, but as long as the Soviet Union existed, this was virtually impossible. For that reason, one of our first actions, on winning independence, was to pass a series of laws making this possible, as well as discussing the question with the governments of the countries in which the largest numbers had settled.

The policy brought immediate success: in the course of the three-year period up to 1995, some 27,000 Kazakh families – that is, more than 123,000 people – were able to return. The policy continues today, even though the numbers involved have begun to decline. This decline is understandable: for many of those left outside Kazakhstan, the decision to return is difficult; many of the original emigrants are now old or have since died. However strong the ties to the homeland, returning is no small matter, especially for those who have their work, family and homes abroad. Nevertheless, the important thing is that all of them know that if one day, they want – or indeed need – to return to Kazakhstan, then it *will* welcome them back. That is how it should be. It would be wrong to try to force the process.

Overall, though, taking both immigration and emigration into account, only slightly more people are now leaving Kazakhstan than are coming to it. The positive tendency is expected to continue as the economic and political situation in the country further stabilises. The numbers are also being boosted by a further tendency: that of re-emigration, namely the return to Kazakhstan of Russians, Ukrainians and members of other national groups who have tried life in their historical homeland and found that it has not worked out for them. The Kazakh government has done everything to help them settle back in the places in Kazakhstan where they used to live. We have seen this with the recovery of some of our metallurgical plants; no sooner do we start being able to pay normal wages, than Russians start returning to work here. Increasingly, it is economics rather than politics which is the decisive factor in migration. As the economic situation in Kazakhstan improves, so this trend will increase.

CHAPTER NINE

THE DIFFERENT FACES
OF THE CIS

THE period since the collapse of the Soviet Union has shown us one thing: it would be much easier for us to work our way out of crisis if political ambitions and unproductive games could be eliminated within the CIS, and if the CIS countries could find a way of pooling their efforts. Over the decades and, indeed, centuries, our economies have become very closely inter-twined; it would be absurd to sever the links between them just because the former members of the Soviet Union have since become sovereign states. It is also against the prevailing mood at the end of the twentieth century. Most countries in the world, guided by common sense and often conceding some of their sovereignty, are in fact moving towards integration of some form or another, not breaking apart.

From the very beginning, Kazakhstan understood the large degree of integration within the single economy of the Soviet Union. Among the states, the closest ties were between Russia and Kazakhstan, Russia and Ukraine, and Russia and Belarus. This reality pushed us to propose a union of these four republics in 1990, but it was rejected by Gorbachev. The aim was to maintain the single economic space and retain the links between enterprises, consumers and suppliers. Indeed, this was formally declared in the Belovezhski documents signed at the end of 1991 and in the speeches of the various Presidents and Ministers from Russia, Ukraine and Belarus. It was said that the time had come at last for genuinely normal economic relations between independent, sovereign states.

In practice, the reverse happened. Following the end of the Soviet Union, the republics moved away from each other and retreated further and further within their own borders. Each began to develop different laws and conflicting constitutions. Each became convinced that it would be richer on its own than as part of the union.

The initial desire of all the republics to continue using a common currency, the rouble, was also dictated by pragmatic considerations. Everyone understood that the manufactured goods which we produced in the former Soviet Union were not good enough to compete on the world market. For that reason we needed to keep the rouble zone as a way of selling our products. The only things which we could hope to sell outside were our raw materials. This was the case not merely for Kazakhstan, but for all the republics.

It did not stop the various governments from hoping. Ukraine, for example, was optimistic of selling in the West rolled metal from metallurgical plants which it had previously sold to Kazakhstan, Uzbekistan and other republics. It did not succeed. And even the republics to which it used to sell began to build plants for themselves instead. In Kazakhstan, for example, we set up a factory capable of producing 20,000 pipes of different diameters every year. So Ukraine, of course, lost its previous share of the Kazakh market, and its production fell.

There were many other such examples. During the Soviet years, Kazakhstan used to buy its supplies of tinned vegetables from Moldova. However, since we grow enough of our own vegetables, we simply decided to built our own plant and can our own. It was the same with wine. Once we used to import from Georgia or elsewhere in the Caucasus, but since we grow grapes as well, we started to make our own wine instead.

However, the problem over the last few years has been more than just a matter of the breakdown in ties between the constituent republics of the Soviet Union. Its effects have been compounded by a complete change in the organisation of the economy. During the Communist years, the state-planning body, *Gossnab*, would order factories what to produce and to whom they should deliver it. The factory directors just had to do as they were told. With the end of Communism, the factory bosses wanted to be free of such commands and become independent, so they stopped taking orders from the respective ministries which used to control them and started doing what they wanted. A number of directors managed to become very rich, as they transferred what had been owned by the state to themselves. It was not planned that way; it was simply the result of the chaos which reigned at that time. This continued all the way through 1992.

Some people wrongly see the economic consequences of the break-up of the Soviet Union as little more than a continuation of the process which had begun a couple of years earlier with the end of *Comecon*, the Soviet-led Communist trading bloc. But you cannot compare relations between Kazakhstan and Russia with those of either say, Poland or Hungary, with Russia. The Soviet Union was one state and one organism. Everything was done so that raw materials would be mined in one place, processed in a second and the machinery to do so manufactured in a third, each of them perhaps as many as several thousand kilometres from the other. Some 93 per cent of the Kazakh economy was controlled by the Soviet-level ministries in Moscow. It was these ministries which allocated subsidies to the factories and gave them money for investment. Virtually the same was true in Ukraine and Belarus as well. During the 1980s, for example, only a quarter of Kazakhstan's budget came from the republic itself. The remainder came from Moscow.

To some extent, the political break-up triggered a push towards isolationism by the leaders of several of the republics and by their political élites. This was particularly the case in Russia after Yegor Gaidar and his team of economists took charge of the economy at the beginning of 1992. They were all young men, fresh out of their various theoretical institutes, who did not know how the Soviet economy had worked in practice and the degree of inter-dependence of its constituent parts. They simply did not know Kazakhstan and the other republics.

Their argument was a simple, if not simplistic, one: Russia's economy was far larger than that of the other republics and (with the exception of Kazakhstan) was much richer in resources of energy and other raw materials. As a result, Russia was subsidising them. Therefore, if Russia severed links with the other republics, its own people would live much better. Until recently, it was an argument which had enjoyed wide support in Russia.

However, reality showed that Russia has actually lost as much if not more than its neighbours as a result of the break-up of the Union and people are now beginning to realise that. A few concrete examples are enough to prove the point: take the power stations of Siberia and the Urals which used to receive 40 million tonnes of coal a year from the Ekibastuz field in Kazakhstan. With the break-down of the old ties between republics, the deliveries stopped, which meant that the Russians had to invest billions of dollars in developing their own coal fields to provide the fuel to keep these power stations working. The same was true of the textile plants in the European regions which every year used to receive 80,000 to 100,000 tonnes of Kazakh wool. They, too, stopped receiving the raw materials they needed and began to close down.

Now, people are at last talking again about re-integration, about the creation of joint ventures, trans-national companies and trusts. This is not new; I have been urging it since before the end of the Soviet Union. But it is gathering pace and there is now the serious possibility of recreating this single economic area, like the European Union or the North American Free Trade Area (NAFTA), in which goods, services and labour are able to circulate freely.

Another question is how open our economies should be to the outside world. Certainly, a completely closed economy cannot grow and develop. However, at the same time, we must be careful that it is not swamped by imports from the more developed countries of the West. This means, in the short term, that we should protect our industries against foreign competition. Instead, we have been doing the opposite, just letting foreign goods in freely. Belatedly, we have now started imposing quotas and customs duties to clamp down on imports and give a chance for our domestic consumer goods producers to develop. Maybe, at least for the moment, the quality of the goods is not very high, but it will certainly improve. It also helps keep our factories running and provides work for our people.

My conviction of the need for economic re-integration explains why, at each of the regular quarterly meetings of the CIS, I have been putting forward the question of adopting a CIS charter. In the Belovezhski document signed at the end of 1991, it is written that the CIS is not a state nor a supra-national organisation. So what is it, then? And who, according to the charter, can be a member, what are their responsibilities and how can they be carried out?

The charter has never been adopted because some of the members of the CIS have never clarified their attitude to the organisation: Ukraine, under Leonid Kravchuk, the country's first post-independence President, was always against any formalisation of the role of the CIS, and was sometimes joined by others such as the Caucasian republics and Moldova. Every session was marred by major arguments between Russia and Ukraine, with the result that documents were never signed. Or, if they were, they were signed by some states and not by the others and never really came into operation. However, all of Central Asia was in favour, as was Belarus.

The only body to be created was a Co-ordinating-Consultative Committee, which was set up in 1992. It used to invite all the heads of state to its sessions, pass out documents and prepare agendas for our meetings, but it did little else. A major omission was that there was no body which tried to harmonise legislation. Each state instead began to set up its own rules on taxes, on customs duties and its own laws on financial activity.

Nevertheless, there are grounds for optimism. The replacement of Kravchuk by Leonid Kuchma as Ukrainian leader in spring 1994 brought about a radical change in the country's policies. Kravchuk was politically stronger, but Kuchma is a more practical man, who has worked in industry and understands life better than his predecessor. Almost at the same time, there were elections in Belarus which also brought a new President, Alexander Lukashenko. Both have supported greater integration within the CIS, including retaining and strengthening relations with Russia.

During the course of 1994, we also made some progress on the working of the CIS, signing agreements to create an economic union and an inter-state economic committee, made up of representatives from all the states. Nevertheless, much more remains to be done.

It is possible to look in different ways at the events of August 1991: Zbigniew Brzezinski, the former US National Security Adviser, wrote that he had devised a scheme to break up the Soviet Union a long time ago and that it had finally succeeded; Ronald Reagan, the former American President, also maintained that he had worked out plans for the break-up of the Union. As a result, many Americans have come to the conclusion that they must act as victors and treat us as the defeated.

It could be said that the collapse of the Soviet Union started with the Solidarity movement in Poland and with the help that was given to tear Poland away from the Soviet bloc. There is also no doubting the help provided by Pope John Paul II; he said as much to me during a meeting we had. As I have discussed in earlier chapters, a major role was also played by subjective factors, in particular the intense personal rivalry between Gorbachev and Yeltsin which made any compromise virtually impossible.

After the failed *coup* and the Belovezhski agreement, Yeltsin demonstrated that Russia was on the path towards democracy and the creation of a market economy, that it was renouncing threats and reducing its strategic weaponry. Many in the West believe that if there is democracy and market economics in Russia, then the same will be true in the surrounding areas. It is difficult to argue against such a view. Certainly, a democratic and market-oriented Russia would be in the interests of Kazakhstan. Indeed, we could not hope for better.

For this reason, after the break-up of the Soviet Union, many Western policy makers were convinced that the main thing was to help Russia to stand on its feet again, and that, if they succeeded, recovery in the other former Soviet republics would follow swiftly. However, during the course of 1993 and 1994, they began to change their position. A major part in this change was played by the bloody conflict with the Russian parliament in October 1993, when Yeltsin used tanks to blast his hard-line Communist opponents out of their headquarters in the White House on the banks of the Moscow River.

I remember meeting Yeltsin at the time. It was 7 September and tension was already building dangerously. After formal talks during the day, I went back to his home in the evening. Naturally we talked about the worsening crisis.

'Boris Nikolayevich,' I told him. 'I think that you should go easy. There could be bloodshed.'

He looked at me, frankly, and said: 'We will squeeze them out peacefully and put an end to it.'

I really believe that was his intention. Yeltsin wanted simply to step up the pressure on his opponents so that they would understand that they were in the wrong and leave it at that. He said the same again on 21 September at a meeting of the CIS held on the same day that he issued his decree formally disbanding parliament. We spoke for more than an hour, and it was clear that he did not intend to use tanks to fire on the White House. In the end, things turned out very differently. The government was not ready to defend itself, so when a mob attacked and stormed the mayor of Moscow's office, things quickly got out of hand, leaving Yeltsin little alternative but to use force.

But the dramatic events of October 1993 paled beside that of the Russian election and referendum of December 1993. Although Yeltsin narrowly secured support for a new constitution which considerably enhanced his powers, the result of the parliamentary election gave cause for concern not just within Russia but also across the world: almost one in four voters backed the extreme nationalist Liberal Democratic Party of Vladimir Zhirinovsky which openly called for the restoration of the Soviet Union. The Communists led by Gennady Zyuganov also did well.

Although Yeltsin refused to allow either into government, there is no doubt that he tried to cut the ground from under their feet in the months that followed by slowing his reform programme. His success was limited: after the parliamentary elections of December 1995, the Communists emerged as by far the strongest party, although Zhirinovsky's support was halved. One of the most alarming acts of the new Communist-dominated parliament was a vote in March 1996 formally refusing to recognise the break-up of the Soviet Union.

The Chechen war, which erupted at the end of 1994, and the enormous bloodshed it caused, only added to Yeltsin's problems.

These dramatic events in Russia changed the relationship between the former Soviet republics. It is clear that unity is our only protection in the future against Fascist and nationalistic intoxication and inter-state conflicts. The best kind of unity and trust is through economics, through trade. If I trade with you and have an economic interest in your continuing existence then I will not do anything to destabilise your country. Shared economic interest between Kazakhstan and Russia, Uzbekistan and the other republics is the fundamental basis on which we can build a normal community of interests.

It is for this reason that I have been urging the members of the CIS to integrate further ever since the break-up of the Soviet Union. Seeing how the proposals which I made came to little, I began to look for alternative solutions. This necessarily meant focusing on our immediate neighbours in Central Asia.

As a first result, in July 1993, Kazakhstan signed an agreement with Uzbekistan on measures to deepen integration of the economies of the two republics for the period from 1994 until 2000. Then, in January 1994, Islam Karimov, the Uzbek President, and I signed a treaty to turn the territory of the two countries into a single economic space. Kyrgyzstan joined a month later.

Just over a year later, on 30 April, 1995, the Central Asian Bank for Co-operation and Development was founded in the city of Chollon-Ate in Kyrgyzstan. An International Council of the three republics was created, and its working body, the Executive Committee. We now have an inter-state bank with US$9 million start-up capital for the financing of joint projects and have begun work on a five-year programme for co-ordinating the economies of the three countries.

For example, if it is decided to build a car assembly in Uzbekistan, then Kazakhstan will provide, say, the rubber, the tyres and the non-ferrous metal; Kyrgyzstan can provide something else. There is also potential for co-operation in other sectors such as pharmaceuticals or making motors for household appliances. Each project implemented would be owned by all three states, and they would take equal shares in the enterprises.

Among other plans under consideration, we are talking about building a giant airport for all three states near Almaty, because this is a very good meridian to be on: flights from Japan to Europe can come via Kazakhstan rather than via Moscow. We are also considering further ways of inter-state harmonising, such as mutual recognition of qualifications and diplomas awarded in the member countries and free movement of citizens. On the technological front, we are aiming to step-up mutual co-operation along the same lines as EU countries in order to help us regain our place internationally. After that, we plan to move on to the next stage of drawing up political, economic and defence agreements between the various states.

The three republics make a good fit. We are all bound together by similar languages and culture: one million Kazakhs live in Uzbekistan and the same number again in Kyrgyzstan. We have also a number of Uzbeks living in Kazakhstan. Since the break-up of the Soviet Union, our three countries have adopted different currencies and begun to build borders between one another, but no one seems to have stopped to consider what the point was. We should have been trading with one another instead. So, I persuaded the Kyrgyz and Uzbek leaders to sign agreements and pull down the customs barriers between us.

Tajikistan and Turkmenistan, the two other Central Asian republics, have so far stayed away from our union. Tajikistan's absence is not surprising, given the chaos in which it has been enveloped over the last few years as a result of the protracted civil war raging there. As Farsi-speakers, the Tajiks are also culturally different from the Turkic peoples of our three republics.

In the case of Turkmenistan, the reasons are different. Turkmenistan is in a very different situation and has set off on a separate path of development from the rest of us. Once the poorest of the Soviet republics, Turkmenistan has huge reserves of coal and gas to develop, which in the long run could make it one of the richest states of the CIS. However, the country also has an authoritarian form of government under which all economic and political power remains in the hands of the state – or rather one man, President Sapurmurat Niyazov. I have known Niyazov for 20 years and teased him about the 'personality cult' he has established, as part of which he has filled the capital with monuments to himself.

'You're not Lenin,' I once told him.

'They can do what they like with the monuments after I die, but let them stay there for the time being,' he replied.

Necessarily, though, joining a union of the type which we envisage would mean Turkmenistan opening up its economy; this, in turn, would mean the end of its current political regime.

Some critics have claimed that the progress which we have made towards regional co-operation and integration somehow constitutes a barrier to integration within the CIS as a whole. The Russians, in particular, warned that they would only open their border with Kazakhstan if we closed ours with the rest of Central Asia. Their argument was that arms, drugs and contraband were coming through Tajikistan. This is absurd, of course. Opening the borders does not mean that you cannot have special controls on criminals. Indeed, our borders are so vast that it is virtually impossible to close all the roads running across them, anyway. If we opened to Russia then we should open to the South as well. What was wrong with the Uzbeks going to Siberia and trading there, bartering their grapes and water melons for oil and other goods?

Far from hurting the CIS, the agreements which we have made with Uzbekistan and Kyrgyzstan have actually furthered integration. While other CIS leaders have just been talking and signing documents, we have actually taken concrete actions in order to set a more vital, active example. The CIS charter states explicitly that there is no prohibition on bilateral or regional alliances. In any case, this was not a trilateral alliance as such; we signed our agreement openly and made clear that any other state was free to join. For instance, if Azerbaijan and Georgia wanted to join our union later, we would have no objections. The progress which we have made also attracted some unlikely admirers: even a delegation from Latvia came to study the principles on which we were integrating and to see if there were any lessons which they could apply to their own relations with their neighbours, Estonia and Lithuania.

Just because two or three states are working together does not mean that they are adopting a stance against any other countries. Kazakhstan has since signed bilateral agreements to form a customs union with Russia and Belarus. To accuse us of separatism was absurd. It should also be remembered that the states have very specific regional problems and other matters to resolve pertaining to the use of common energy capacities, water resources and other fundamental sectors which we share, such as transport and communications.

However significant the process of integration within Central Asia, one thing is clear: no one is talking about creating some kind of single Central Asian state, a new Turkestan. All our states have only just declared their independence; there would be no point in giving that up and merging with each other. What we are talking about instead is finding a way to co-ordinate our activities for the good of our citizens without giving up our hard-won sovereignty.

CHAPTER TEN

FORWARD TO A NUCLEAR-FREE FUTURE

To GENERATIONS of Kazakhs, the region around Semipalatinsk in the steppes is known as the birthplace of Abai, one of our most renowned poet-philosophers. Abai enjoys an important place in Kazakh culture thanks to the considerable amount of literature which he translated from Russian, German and English into the Kazakh language and his ethnography of the Kazakhs. It was the birthplace, too, of the poet Auezov, who wrote the epic of the Kazakh people. Over the last half century, Semipalatinsk has also become synonymous with one of the world's worst man-made ecological disasters.

In 1949 the Soviet army carried out its first atmospheric test at the Semipalatinsk site. Among those who were watching was Andrei Sakharov. Later one of the Soviet Union's leading human rights campaigners, Sakharov was, at the time, a young physicist working at a top-secret outpost known only as 'the installation'. In his memoirs, Sakharov recalls the first tests with a growing horror, describing how he surveyed the scorched landscape and dead birds and heard how people in the area were dying of radiation poisoning. Later, he was to estimate that thousands of people in Kazakhstan would suffer illness as a result of the tests. The experience was one of the main factors behind his transformation into a dissident and forthright opponent of the Soviet Union's military plans.

It is difficult to overestimate the sheer destruction which these tests caused to Kazakhstan. It was nothing less than genocide, the wiping out by the Soviet government of its own people. The republic's government were aware of what was happening, of course, but there was nothing they could do to stop it. Over the course of 41 years, there were 752 explosions, 26 in the atmosphere, 78 at ground-level and the rest underground. The whole city shook when the nuclear charges went off. At that time, I was working in Karaganda, some 50 kilometres away; even at that distance we still felt the shock-wave.

I had a friend who used to live in Ayaguz, near the test site. He described how at midday, when the sun was blazing down, a second sun, just as bright, appeared in the sky. Most of the people in this densely-populated area did not understand what was happening. Suddenly it began to snow but the flakes were radioactive.

I met another man born near Semipalatinsk. He was one of four children: his sister went mad, one of his brothers suffered from anaemia, the other committed suicide. There are thousands more like him in the area. Even today, children are still being born without arms and legs and with disabilities of all sorts. All the time, the Third Department of the Soviet ministry of health was running a secret hospital in Semipalatinsk in order to monitor the effect of the radioactivity on local people. For decades they refused to hand us the documents revealing how our people had suffered.

There were even special rural settlements of 50 or so people whom they used as guinea pigs; they would bring them a crate of vodka and 100 roubles each.

'Just wait here until we come back,' they used to tell the people. Then, after the explosion, they would come back and see what the radiation had done to them.

As many as half a million people suffered the effects of the tests either directly or indirectly. It was only after 1988, when Gorbachev's policy of *glasnost* was sufficiently advanced, that we could begin to penetrate the wall of security which surrounded the whole issue. Only then could we fully understand the extent of the crime which had been committed against us.

It was not just Semipalatinsk, either. According to the records, at least 20 smaller charges were detonated over the years for 'economic' reasons: sometimes geologists prospecting for oil used nuclear explosions to help them in their search; other times they were used to build underground gas storages. The details were known only to a small circle of people.

Nor was it just a matter of nuclear weapons. Almost our entire republic, from the Urals to the Irtysh River, was turned into a giant test site for this or that weapon by the Soviet military; 15 million hectares in all. Ballistic missiles, anti-ballistic missiles, laser weapons and so on, they tested them all. In the middle of the Aral Sea, on the Vozrozhdyeniya Island, they had a test site for bacteriological weapons. Further environmental damage was caused by Baikonur, the main launch site for the Soviet space programme. Kazakhstan was turned into a giant rubbish dump.

Even after Gorbachev came to power in 1985 and the gradual democratisation of society began, the central defence agencies in Moscow continued to behave as if their word was law. I remember one occasion, when I was Prime Minister, one of the leaders of the Soviet Council of Ministers telephoning me.

'Nursultan Abishevich, on the suggestion of the defence sector, a decision has been taken to build a new testing range in the Taldy-Kurgan region,' he said. 'The Central Committee of the Kazakh Communist Party has also given its agreement. We now urgently need some land. Could you please organise for 10 to 12,000 hectares to be allocated and also be ready to receive a delegation of generals and specialists who will make the concrete preparations.'

'Excuse me,' I asked, 'but do you actually have a concrete resolution of the Central Committee of the Soviet Communist Party and of the government? And did you consult anyone at all in Taldy-Kurgan? And why am I, the leader of the government of Kazakhstan, only hearing about this now for the first time?'

'What does it matter?' the official replied angrily. 'The project has been drawn up and the Central Committee has agreed. Simply sign the document when we send it to you and do as you are told.'

But I, too, was now angry.

'I am sorry,' I said, 'but I am not going to sign such a document. What's more, I am going to formally ask for it to be reconsidered.'

'You just try,' he replied and hung up.

I immediately called Kolbin, who had just been appointed Kazakh Communist Party leader.

'Gennady Vasilyevich, I have just been informed that Moscow has decided to build a new test site in the republic and that you gave your agreement. Is it true?'

'There was such a conversation,' he said, 'but as I recall, it was not about building a new site, but rather extending an old one. Why are you interested, anyway? Is there some problem?'

Of course there was a problem, and I tried to convince him how undesirable the whole project was. Kolbin did not attempt to disagree with me, but at the same time he made it clear that I could not rely on any support from him.

'Well, if you really are opposed to the new site, just try and stop it then,' he said, ending the conversation in much the same way as the man from Moscow had done.

I realised that it was now entirely up to me. I had a number of conversations with senior officials in the central military agencies and with secretaries of the Communist Party Central Committee, but to no avail. I also tried to speak to Gorbachev, but was unable to reach him.

It was then that I tried rather more unconventional means. At that time one of the leaders of the Taldy-Kurgan region was Seilbek Shaukhamanov, a man whom I had known for years and whom I was sure that I could trust. I telephoned him and told him that we had to stop this plan.

'Seilbek,' I said, 'you can do whatever you want as long as you make sure that the rumour begins to go around that they are planning to build this test site. Also, in the next few days, make sure that some kind of spontaneous mass meeting takes place to protest against the new site. If the local people appear to be angry enough about this, it may be just enough to stop it.'

'Alright,' he agreed reluctantly. 'But you know that we could lose our jobs over this.'

'But if you don't do as I say, I will fire you myself,' I retorted.

I must say, that despite his reservations, Shaukhamanov did his job rather well. Soon both we, and the 'competent organs' in Moscow, began to receive information about growing popular discontent and social tension in Taldy-Kurgan about the planned new site. Although the danger posed by the site was real, the popular reaction was, of course, exaggerated. Nevertheless, I sent off a number of messages to various different bodies in Moscow, citing the discontent and again questioning the rationale behind the building of the new test site. It was then that I finally obtained the response which

I wanted: the authorities changed their mind and cancelled the project.

On 24 April, 1990, the Supreme Soviet of Kazakhstan elected me as President, the first in the history of our republic. One of my first acts was to demand the closure of the Semipalatinsk site.

Gorbachev, Nikolai Ryzhkov, the Soviet Prime Minister, and other leading members of the military-industrial complex were horrified at my stand. 'What are you doing?' they asked. 'Let us come down there and we will talk to the people and explain everything to them.' But it was already too late. I was determined to stop this destruction once and for all.

Popular feeling against the tests had been growing within Kazakhstan as the full extent of the damage which they had done became clear. Thanks to the growing liberalisation of the Soviet political system, it was also now possible for this discontent to become more focused. Thus the Nevada-Semipalatinsk movement, named after the two superpower test sites, was set up.

Ostensibly, like other such popular movements which sprang up around that time across the Soviet Union, Nevada-Semipalatinsk was an independent group. However, behind the scenes, I was doing everything I could to encourage its formation because I knew that public pressure would be a key weapon in forcing the Kremlin to stop the tests – or at least to shift them elsewhere. I also ensured that the movement had a suitably charismatic leader, in the form of Olzhas Suleimenov. A poet and one of Kazakhstan's best-known cultural figures, Suleimenov had stood as a candidate in the spring 1989 elections to the Congress of People's Deputies, the Soviet Union's first democratic parliament. To his surprise, he had been beaten by a simple building worker, and was looking for a role to play. I knew his popular standing would make him the perfect leader for the movement and persuaded him to stand.

My confidence in the strength of public opinion was soon vindicated. Although the Soviet military carried out yet another test at Semipalatinsk in October 1989, the adverse public reaction was so great that even Gorbachev had to take notice. It was decided to stage the next few tests in Novaya Zemlya, an Arctic Island off the coast of Russia. But still no formal decision had been made to close the Semipalatinsk site. The military's plans called for three more tests in Kazakhstan, and there was still the danger that they might yet carry them out.

The attempted *coup* of August 1991 and its failure completely transformed the situation. With the central powers dramatically weakened, I now had the authority which I needed to end all testing once and for all. On 29 August, I issued a presidential decree forbidding further nuclear tests of any sort to be held on the territory of Kazakhstan.

The Kazakh republic has already 'fulfilled its duty for the creation of a nuclear potential that ensured strategic military parity between the USSR and USA,' I wrote in the document. Therefore, taking into consideration the demands of the Kazakh people, it was deemed expedient to close the testing ground immediately. Under the terms of the decree, the site would be transformed into a Union-republican research centre.

There had been enormous pressure on me not to go ahead with such a step. Starting in 1989, I was summoned several times to Moscow to the offices of high-ranking officers in the Communist Party and the government and asked to give my agreement to allowing more nuclear tests in Kazakhstan. Kolbin agreed, they said, why won't you? When I discussed the matter with Gorbachev, he pointed out that if I, a Kazakh, signed, it would greatly help to calm public opinion. I was also warned that I might be removed from my job as Prime Minister if I continued to be difficult. I did not listen either to their arguments or to their threats.

Powerful people within the military-industrial complex continued to put pressure on me even after I had signed my anti-nuclear decree, but when I thought of the more than 500 tests which had already been carried out and all the damage which they had done, I knew that I had no choice. Half a million people had been given potentially damaging doses of radiation because of these tests and what compensation had they received? Nothing. Instead, the authorities had lied and withheld information about what was really going on and about the damage to people's health. As for the cities of Semipalatinsk and Kurchatov, they remained wretched, poverty-ridden places. The contrast with Las Vegas and other cities in the area around the American test site in the Nevada desert could not have been greater. There was no doubt that the Soviet authorities were completely indifferent to the fate of their own people.

Given the new political situation, however, it was clear that the leadership in Moscow had no real power to stop me now. Already, the same day as my decree, Yevgeny Shaposhnikov, the newly appointed Defence Minister, announced that the three further blasts which they had planned for Semipalatinsk would be shifted to the Arctic test site of Novaya Zemlya.

The fate of Semipalatinsk was not the only nuclear problem which we had to confront. There was also the question of what to do with the huge number of nuclear weapons which were situated on Kazakh soil.

Although the Union formally continued to exist after the failed *coup*, no one had any illusions that it would last long. On the one hand, Yeltsin was taking part in talks on an agreement to maintain the Union in the form of a Union of Sovereign States, but on the other, he gave the order that Russia stop financing the Soviet ministries and dissolve the Soviet National Bank. Meanwhile, the authority of both Gorbachev and of the Soviet-level political structures in general was dropping. The key question was: what was going to happen to the Soviet Union's nuclear arsenal?

It was a question which preoccupied not only those of us within the former Soviet Union; the United States and its Western allies were also highly apprehensive about the future. Amid fears that the Union could degenerate into chaos, they were worried that some of the weapons might be acquired by unstable Middle-Eastern regimes. Worse still, they might find their way into the hands of terrorists.

The Western position was clear: determined to prevent any proliferation, they wanted Russia to inherit all the Soviet Union's weapons. It was a position which, necessarily, appealed to the Russian authorities who were busy asserting themselves as the legal successor of the USSR. However, for us, it could not be quite as a simple as that.

Kazakhstan, as one of the four 'nuclear' republics, was of special interest to the West. It was here, on our vast territory, that the Soviet Union had based some of its most deadly inter-continental nuclear missiles: SS-18s, 104 of them each with 10 warheads, making a total of more than 1,000. Suddenly, Western leaders began queuing up to visit us, in order to try and find out what our policy would be.

One of the first to come was Margaret Thatcher, who stopped over briefly in Almaty at the beginning of September 1991. Although no longer British Prime Minister, she was still a very influential figure. She was followed the next month by Roland Dumas, the French Foreign Minister, and Hans-Dietrich Genscher, his German counterpart.

The stream of Western visitors all wanted to know how Kazakhstan would behave after the *coup*: whether or not we would declare our independence. Ukraine, Belarus, Kyrgyzstan and several other republics had already taken that step and they wanted to know if we would follow. There was little doubt that their concern was linked with the fate of the weapons. I responded by assuring them that we understood the sensitive nature of the problem and would do everything to ensure that the entire arsenal remained under centralised control.

I have different memories from each of the visits. I was particularly impressed by Lady Thatcher. She was on her way to Tokyo and her private jet needed to refuel. The pilot had planned to land in Tashkent, the Uzbek capital, but she wanted to come to Almaty to see me instead. I was delighted. It was decided that we would meet at the airport.

What a journey I had to get there! The day before I had been extraordinarily busy and I had had to work through the night and into the morning. A couple of hours or so before she was due to arrive, I finally had a couple of hours free and I decided to have a snooze on the sofa. My bodyguards knew about the visit but did not dare to wake me up. In the end I woke up myself and saw to my horror that we only had 40 minutes before Lady Thatcher was due to land. My driver drove to the airport as though we were in a Formula One race, but even then we only just made it on time. It was only when I reached the VIP hall of the airport that I finally relaxed. It is no exaggeration to say that I had never rushed so much before in my life.

Lady Thatcher, however, was calm and composed. Despite the fact that she had been sitting on an aeroplane for seven hours, she was charming and extremely energetic. She was accompanied by her son Mark and another official.

As soon as we began to talk, I understood that she was familiar not only with my speeches and with articles and papers which I had written, but also with what was more broadly going on within Kazakhstan and the rest of the CIS. I began to understand that, in coming to see me, she was assuming for herself a kind of mission as a diplomatic plenipotentiary on behalf of the Western countries in order to learn about the nuclear weapon situation in Kazakhstan.

She spoke to me with great warmth about Gorbachev, though at the same time acknowledging the considerable mistakes that he had made. She also spoke about Yeltsin as the leader of Russia. To be honest, I had the feeling that she was very sad about the collapse of the Soviet Union.

We spoke for only 90 or so minutes, but it was enough time to acquire a very favourable impression of her. When she spoke to journalists there, she praised me for having always spoken out in favour of integration as the way of ensuring peace and stability. 'Nazarbayev is now one of the leaders who can unite the Union,' she said.

Another visitor who left a strong impression was the German, Genscher. He agreed with Lady Thatcher on the importance of establishing democracy in Kazakhstan and the other republics. But he had no illusions about how difficult it would be for Russia, in particular, to become a truly democratic country and to behave fairly towards the smaller states which surrounded it. He gave as an ideal the way in which West Germany – and later, the united Germany – behaved towards the other countries of the then European Community. Although Germany was far larger in territory, financial and political power than say, Belgium or the Netherlands, it always adhered to the principle that all the states within the community had equal rights.

For this reason, Genscher maintained that Russia should also declare itself to be no more than the equal of the other former Soviet republics and reflect this in its behaviour towards them. We discussed other issues, too, such as the fate of the ethnic Germans who had been deported to Kazakhstan by Stalin, 900,000 of whom still lived in our republic. Genscher, too, was concerned about the nuclear issue.

Necessarily, however, the main talks on this front were with the Americans. On the evening of 17 December, 1991, James Baker, the US Secretary of State, arrived in Kazakhstan as part of a whirlwind tour which also took in the three other nuclear republics – Belarus, Ukraine and Russia. He was accompanied by Robert Strauss, the American ambassador. I invited Baker, his wife and Strauss back to my home to meet my family. The atmosphere was warm and friendly: as we sat eating at the table we sang some Kazakh, Russian and American songs. We men then went to another room to talk, eventually ending up in the *banya*, the Russian steam bath. For the Americans, it must have been very exotic to sit discussing world political problems in a room full of steam at 90° Celsius, but for us it was absolutely normal. Fortunately, though, Baker seemed to enjoy the whole thing.

I tried to lay out Kazakhstan's position as clearly as possible: since all the other republics had declared their sovereignty and independence, Kazakhstan had no alternative but to do the same. However, I insisted that it would be wrong to see this as an attempt by us to stake a claim to the nuclear weapons on our territory. We were realists; we knew how expensive it would be to maintain these weapons. There was also the practical problem of the necessary expertise, insofar as the missiles had been built in Russia and Ukraine, and almost all the maintenance personnel were from there.

Nevertheless, we were not prepared simply to renounce these weapons without getting something in return – in particular, security guarantees. During the conversation, Baker warned us that three American missiles were targeted at each one of ours. 'I am not frightened of that and anyway it is not the point,' I replied. 'We will decide everything on an equal basis. First of all, we need to know what Kazakhstan will get in return for dismantling these weapons.' In all, though, it was a positive discussion. Baker said that President Bush would invite me for an official visit to Washington and we could discuss the issue there. I must say that Baker carried out his promises. He was an exemplary Secretary of State.

After several years, James Baker resigned. In April 1996 I invited him to visit Kazakhstan. We spent our time fishing and horse riding, as well as reminiscing about the events of 1991. He, in return, invited me to visit his birthplace, Texas, which I promised to do one day…

Deciding the fate of the weapons was one of the most important issues on the agenda of the meeting of republican leaders a few days later in December 1991 in Almaty, at which we formally set up the Commonwealth of Independent States. In principle, we agreed to create a joint military command to control all the armed forces and nuclear weapons. And we named Shaposhnikov, the Soviet Defence Minister, as temporary head of the unified military command. The question was due to be decided for good at a further meeting in Minsk, the Belarussian capital, set for 30 December.

The Minsk meeting effectively confirmed the decision. All 27,000 of the Soviet Union's nuclear warheads were to be put under a single authority which was to be called the United Strategic Forces of the CIS, with headquarters in Moscow. Shaposhnikov was confirmed as commander. The decision on the use of these forces would be taken jointly by the Presidents of the four republics on whose territory the weapons were situated. For this reason, we established a series of special 'hot lines' linking the four of us Presidents. We each had a secret code; in order to fire the weapons each of us had to give his code, effectively giving each of us the right of veto.

Yet there were still many issues remaining to be solved. Tying up all the loose ends was to take several years.

It was not until May 1992 that I went to Washington. The US position was essentially unchanged: put simply, they wanted Kazakhstan to renounce its claims to the nuclear weapons still on its territory and to sign the 1968 Nuclear Non-Proliferation Treaty as a non-nuclear state. For us the situation was necessarily more complex.

Kazakhstan had never wanted to become a nuclear power in the first place. Indeed, the republic and its people had paid an enormous price for this status through the damage which they suffered over the decades from the fall-out from the Semipalatinsk tests. There wasn't any doubt that our eventual aim was to become nuclear-free. By my decree on Semipalatinsk, I had closed down one of the two largest nuclear arms test sites in the world.

Yet there was still the problem of our security. It is easy, just a few years later, to forget how potentially unstable the situation was in the immediate aftermath of the break-up of the Soviet Union. Given all the uncertainty about the future of the Commonwealth and about the Russian leadership, we were naturally reluctant to give a formal guarantee to give up the weapons. For this reason, it was not fair of the United States to put us under so much pressure over the issue – much more, in fact, than it had ever put on either India or Pakistan, whose nuclear ambitions had long been well-known. My main aim was to be flexible.

I pointed out in an interview with the *Washington Post* just before my visit to America, that our two largest neighbours, Russia and China, both had nuclear weapons. We had legitimate concerns about their attitudes towards us: as had been shown by the outburst by Pavel Voshchanov, Yeltsin's spokesman, immediately after the failure of the *coup*, there were many influential forces in Russia which had their eyes on large swathes of Northern Kazakhstan. There were also Chinese textbooks which claimed that parts of Siberia and Kazakhstan belonged to China. How was Kazakhstan expected to react?

My conclusion was that, before giving up its weapons, Kazakhstan should be given security guarantees by the United States, China and Russia. The three of them should conclude a non-aggression pact with us which would guarantee Kazakhstan's territorial integrity. Some have tried to ascribe to us a hidden agenda. We did not have one. It was simply a question of national security.

There was another, more legalistic, question concerning the capacity in which Kazakhstan should sign the Non-Proliferation Treaty. America wanted us to adopt the simple formulation of a 'non-nuclear state'. We initially preferred Kazakhstan to be described as a 'republic on which nuclear weapons are temporarily located'. Article nine of the Non-Proliferation Treaty declares that a state which manufactured and exploded nuclear weapons before 1967 is a nuclear state. By this definition Kazakhstan was a nuclear state insofar as weapons had been tested there since 1949. It had also participated in one way or the other in the development and manufacture of nuclear weapons components long before 1967.

We were perfectly prepared to keep to the treaties signed by the former Soviet Union on tactical nuclear missiles and on the reduction of strategic offensive weapons. But even if all sides agreed on the total elimination of nuclear weapons, it would take from 10 to 15 years to implement. And during this time the weapons would still be on Kazakh territory. There was no use in deceiving people by telling them that this republic or that was 'nuclear-free'.

Just a few days before I was due to fly to Washington, there was an important development which helped unblock the situation. After long discussion at a summit on 15 May in Tashkent, the Uzbek capital, six of the CIS states, including both Russia and Kazakhstan, signed a defence pact; under its terms, each signatory was committed to come to the assistance of the others if they were attacked. This made for a qualitative change in the sphere of Kazakhstan's national security. There were also signs of more flexibility on the part of the Americans.

On 17 May, a Sunday, on my way to Washington, I stopped off in Moscow for talks with Yeltsin. I wanted to know his position as far as the weapons on our territory were concerned. Was it in Russia's interests to destroy them or not? It was not only a matter of politeness. Given that we had just signed a treaty on co-operation and mutual assistance, the whereabouts of the missiles on the territories of our two republics was something which the two of us should decide together. It was the first time that I had discussed such complex issues on an international level, and I decided to take a representative of the Russian General Staff with me to Washington.

On that same day, the Kazakh foreign ministry put out a statement confirming the republic's desire to rid itself of nuclear weapons and pledging to join the 1968 Nuclear Non-Proliferation Treaty. 'The prerequisites have been created for Kazakhstan to join the Nuclear Non-Proliferation Treaty as a non-nuclear state,' the statement said. As a courtesy to Baker, I had telephoned the day before to advise him what we were going to announce.

There were still some outstanding details to be resolved. Once I arrived in the US, my talks with President Bush kept being delayed. I remember how Baker came four times that Monday to see me in Blair House, where I was staying. I showed him the agreement which Yeltsin and I had drawn up and asked him to show it to Bush. Russia and Kazakhstan would not move their missiles around, I said, but I also insisted that the two of us, as allies, would decide together whether or not Kazakhstan would give up its nuclear status. All the time the Russian officer was sitting next to me, giving me advice and correcting any mistakes which I made.

In the end, at a breakfast meeting with Baker on Tuesday, I finally signed a letter in which I pledged that Kazakhstan would sign the Nuclear Non-Proliferation Treaty as a 'non-nuclear' state. I also committed Kazakhstan to becoming a signatory to the Strategic Arms Reduction Treaty (START), signed by Mikhail Gorbachev and George Bush at the Moscow summit in July 1991, which required cuts of 38 per cent in the former Soviet arsenal of long-range nuclear missiles, bombers and submarines. When I met Bush, later that day, we were able to agree on a mutually acceptable formula: under its terms, the United States acknowledged Kazakhstan's concern about its security and agreed that, in accordance with the UN charter, it would take all possible measures if Kazakhstan came under threat from aggression.

Some observers accused Kazakhstan of changing its position; well, so had the

Americans. Nevertheless, under the terms of the collective security agreement which we signed in Tashkent, I would not rule out the eventual deployment of weapons on my soil seven years later, once the duration of the START treaty had elapsed. 'Whether or not nuclear weapons will be deployed on the territory of any of the member states will be determined by the situation that exists at a certain historical period in time,' I told a press conference that Wednesday.

Although the nuclear issue was the most difficult one, I also signed other agreements with Bush on various aspects of bilateral relations. All in all, the visit was a success. These agreements were very important for Kazakhstan and the CIS.

I have good memories of this visit and about Bush as a person. He was scrupulous about even small details. When I visited his apartment, I saw some of his grandchildren's toys in one of the rooms. I told him about my grandchildren as well and when I came back to my hotel, I found gifts: a big rubber frog for my grandchildren and a box of tennis balls and a special tennis ball machine for me. I had mentioned only once my interest in tennis, but he had remembered.

Immediately after we signed, Baker flew to Lisbon together with a representative of Kazakhstan. Officials from Russia, Ukraine and Belarus were already waiting there. A few days later, on 23 May, the so-called Lisbon protocols were signed. Under the terms of the six-page document, Kazakhstan, Ukraine and Belarus formally agreed with the United States and Russia to give up the nuclear weapons on their territory by the end of the decade. The ceremony, held in front of a small group of invited guests in a Lisbon hotel, took just six minutes, but there was no doubting its significance. At a stroke, one of the key issues facing the states of the former Soviet Union had been resolved.

Looking back, the decisions which I made that week were clearly difficult ones. Because of Semipalatinsk, Kazakhstan had suffered badly from the effects of nuclear weapons. If only for this reason, we felt that we could not leave the world in fear. This was all the more so because the Western countries saw us as a Moslem country and were worried that our weapons would find their way to other, more radical Islamic states. This fear was heightened by the breakdown of controls on our borders.

Indeed, once talk of Kazakhstan giving up its nuclear weapons began, I was visited by representatives of several Arab states. Some came to me in an official capacity, others non-officially; some with letters, some without. Their basic question was the same: how much money would Kazakhstan need in order to keep these missiles?

It was more than just a matter of weaponry. We could not allow our young state to find itself isolated. Given my determination to attract Western investment to Kazakhstan, I had to give special attention to our relations with the United States and its allies.

It was one thing to agree on general principles, we also had to decide the fate of the missiles themselves. Each missiles was buried 40 metres underground and had a massive infrastructure. According to the CIS agreements, all this was the property of the republic on whose territory it was situated. Now, it was all very well requiring us to destroy these weapons, but they still remained our property and we wanted some compensation for losing them – at the very least, we wanted to be paid the value of the enriched uranium which they contained. We also wanted to keep the equipment.

These negotiation were very long and complicated and were conducted on our side by the Foreign Minister and the Defence Minister. The log-jam was finally broken by the American Senators, Sam Nunn, chairman of the Senate Committee on Armed Services, and Richard Lugar, a member of the Committee on Foreign Relations, who visited Kazakhstan in November 1992. They came up with a plan, the Nunn-Lugar programme, under which the United States committed nearly US$800 million to transfer hundreds of missiles from Kazakhstan, Ukraine and Belarus to Russia for dismantling and to compensate the republics for the weapons-grade uranium in their warheads.

By late 1993, things were beginning to move. That October, Warren Christopher, the American Secretary of State, came to Almaty as part of a visit to all four 'nuclear republics' of the former Soviet Union. The background to the visit was a warm one. The American press was full of quotes from American officials praising Kazakhstan as a model for our Central Asian neighbours and noting the progress we had made in converting our old Soviet state-run economy to private enterprise.

During the talks, I was determined to press home to Christopher how much we still needed help with our security. At one point, I spread a map out on a table to show him how Kazakhstan was surrounded by great powers – Russia to the north, China to the east and Iran to the south. I also told him that I had just returned from China and wanted to establish 'strategic relationships' with all our neighbours. The American press made much of the fact that Iranian President Hashemi Rafsanjani arrived on a visit to Almaty less than an hour after Christopher left. As the Americans drove off to the airport, the streets of the city were already lined with red, white and green Iranian flags in anticipation of Rafsanjani's arrival.

Christopher's visit went well. At the end of his two days in Almaty, I publicly pledged that the Nuclear Non-Proliferation Treaty would be sent to parliament by the end of the year. In return, Christopher announced a package of up to US$140 million in aid for Kazakhstan for the new fiscal year that had just begun, about triple the US$36 million which we had been offered the previous year. The promised US aid included a major programme to help the development of private enterprise and featured a US$15 million fund to 'rehabilitate' the Aral Sea. We were also to receive the first US$84 million of the Nunn-Lugar money. In a sign of the importance which the United States accorded to relations with Kazakhstan, I was invited to a summit with Clinton in early 1994.

To make life easier for American corporations wanting to do business in Kazakhstan, Christopher signed a treaty exempting them from being taxed twice – in Kazakhstan and in the United States – on the profits they made in the country. Before he left, I presented Christopher with a traditional full-length camel hair coat, called a *chapan*, and a matching *kalpak*, a hat.

My pledge was very welcome to the Americans, especially since Christopher had to fly on to Ukraine where changes in President Leonid Kravchuk's policy posed what they saw as a very serious threat. Kravchuk had repeatedly promised to dismantle the arsenal of 1,800 missiles which Ukraine had inherited from the Soviet Union, only to delay the pledge in the face of demands from nationalist groups. A few days before Christopher's arrival, Kravchuk had alarmed the Americans by saying openly that he did not believe that the existing agreements on nuclear weapons required him to destroy them all. The timing of my pledge was seen by commentators as giving Christopher a chance to increase the pressure on him.

But still we were not entirely happy with the guarantees that the Americans were prepared to offer us. I also knew that I would have problems convincing parliament to ratify the agreement. Washington understood our concern and it was decided that Al Gore, the Vice-President, would come to Almaty that December to try and sort out the remaining problems.

How do I remember Christopher? He was self-confident and stubborn when it came to his own opinions and recommendations. For example, after our meeting, literally at the door as he was on his way out, he suggested signing an agreement to dismantle Kazakhstan's nuclear installations and to confirm the country's willingness to sign the Nuclear Non-Proliferation Treaty. I did not object, but I wondered why the Secretary of State was involved in such issues. They were normally settled at a higher level. I therefore pointed out that such matters could be resolved only at a meeting with the US President. Christopher was not happy, but had little alternative but to agree, and left.

The meeting with Gore almost did not happen. Air Force II, with the Vice-President on board, had been due to land in Almaty on the evening of 12 December. A Kazakh state dinner was planned for that evening. However, the airport was covered in fog. After two attempts at landing, and with not enough fuel left for a third attempt, the pilot was forced to land in Bishkek, the capital of neighbouring Kyrgyzstan. Askar Akayev, the Kyrgyz President, had not been expecting Gore until the next day. But he rose to the occasion, bringing forward his own planned state dinner by one day. The next morning the fog lifted and Gore was able to fly in to Almaty safely.

By coincidence, that day had already been set for the Kazakh parliament to vote on ratification of the Non-Proliferation Treaty. After a short time talking with Gore, I broke off and went to address the deputies. The debate was heated and many members of parliament were resolutely opposed, but I convinced them and they eventually backed ratification by 238 votes to one. It was one of the last acts of the outgoing parliament, which on 8 December had voted to dissolve itself and call early elections for a new assembly.

Gore was delighted to hear my news when we resumed talks that afternoon. With the last obstacle gone, he confirmed that we would be receiving the US $84 million in Nunn-Lugar money to help dismantle our arsenal, as well as the other aid. I was invited to go to America on 14 February, 1994 for a summit with Clinton. In return, we signed a framework agreement under which we would begin to dismantle the more than 1,300 strategic weapons which we had inherited from the Soviet Union in 1991. 'Kazakhstan has complied with common sense that is in favour in the world,' I told reporters after the ceremony to sign the aid agreement.

Gore had come with his wife, and during that short visit both of our families got to know each other well; I remember we even sang some Kazakh songs together. For his part, Gore sang 'Jingle Bells'. It all obviously made an impression on him. During a reception at the State Department during my visit to Washington the following February, he asked me to sing again.

The visit itself, my second official one to Washington, went well. Clinton made a strong impression. Among the matters decided, we created a joint economic commission, signed agreements on double taxation, protection of investment and so on. As a result, the United States is now the largest single investor in Kazakhstan.

The final element fell into place on 5 December, 1994 in Budapest, where the United States, Britain and Russia signed a document which gave Kazakhstan the guarantees which we needed. Together they guaranteed our territorial integrity, the unchanging nature of our borders, and ruled out the use of economic pressure against us. And in the case of aggression against us, they agreed they would immediately demand the summoning of the UN Security Council to consider our situation. As a President, I felt that I had done what my people needed.

However, it was not quite the end of the nuclear problem. Under the terms of our membership of the International Atomic Energy Agency in Vienna, we were required to provide a full inventory of all the nuclear material stored on the territory of Kazakhstan.

Around 60 per cent of the reserves of uranium in the former Soviet Union are situated in Kazakhstan, and we also have a factory, the Urba Metallurgical Combine near the city of Ust-Kamenogorsk in eastern Kazakhstan, which makes nuclear fuel for the power stations of all the former republics. Our inventory showed that, in addition to the low-level nuclear waste, some 600 kilograms of highly-enriched uranium were also stored at the plant. According to our specialists, it would have been enough to make more than 20 warheads of considerable power.

As soon as I heard the news, I realised the seriousness of the situation and ordered officials to solve the problem of what to do with this material; our main goal was to avoid it getting into the wrong hands. Their conclusion was clear: reprocessing this material on site was impossible. In order to comply with the NNP Treaty, we would have to transport it to one of the other nuclear powers, which, in effect, meant either

FIG. 26 The 40th anniversary of the opening of the virgin lands. Kunaev, Solomentsev, Brezhnev, Sherbakov, Ashimov, Nazarbayev, Gorbachev.

FIG. 27 At Semipalatinsk's nuclear testing site, September 1993

Fig. 28 With wife, Sarah Alpysovna, 1996.

FIG. 29 With grandchildren, 1993.

FIG. 30 On the ski slopes of Kazakhstan, 1997.

FIG. 31 On the Kazakh steppes, 1996.

Fig. 32 Playing chess with Grand Master Anatoly Karpov, December 1995.

FIG. 33 The Tengiz oilfields. (PHOTO: *Curtesy Chevron Petroleum Inc.*)

Russia or the United States. We first contacted the Russians, telling them in writing how much uranium was there and asking them if they wanted to buy it. In theory, the Russians should have known about this material. After all, the Soviet Union used to be one country and all the records must have been held in one place, presumably in Moscow. However, I had the impression from their reaction that they had simply forgotten about it. They said they did not need it and we were free to dispose of it ourselves.

So, we began talks with the Americans, who were immediately interested. The US defence secretary came to Kazakhstan to discuss the issue. The matter also came up during my meeting with President Clinton in Washington in February 1994. It was decided, after long discussion, that the material would be transported to one of the Americans' installations which had the necessary experience to store and handle this kind of material. We started drawing up plans for how to transport it. We called it 'Operation Sapphire'.

The operation was carried out in conditions of absolute secrecy: for security reasons, it was vital to prevent even the tiniest bit of information about what we were planning leaking out in advance. The whole operation, from its planning to the packing up and transporting of the material, was entrusted to a special committee including representatives from the Kazakh government, our Atomic Energy agency, the Urba Metallurgical Combine and our foreign and security services. On the American side, some 31 officials and nearly 120 tonnes of equipment were involved.

The rest of the world first knew about it in November 1994, when William Perry, the US defence secretary, announced the successful conclusion of 'Operation Sapphire' at a news conference in Washington. Earlier that morning, the last of the material had arrived safely at an American nuclear facility at Oak Ridge, Tennessee.

Some of the reports which appeared in the American press in the following days were somewhat fanciful; if you were to believe them anyone could simply have walked in to the Urba Combine and taken away the uranium. In reality, the factory was a closed one: no one could enter its territory without security clearance and the uranium was kept under special guard. Nevertheless, its presence in Kazakhstan was a worry and we were certainly relieved to be rid of it.

Even more far-fetched was the claim made in some newspapers that we had been threatening to 'sell' the material to Iran if the Americans had not taken it. This was clearly nonsense. No such talks were ever held or even proposed with the Iranians. Indeed, as experts later pointed out, whatever the Iranians' nuclear ambitions, they would have had no interest in buying it. The material stored at Urba was in alloy with beryllium. Extracting uranium from this alloy requires very complicated and expensive technology which Iran simply does not have.

The main message of 'Operation Sapphire' was that relations between the United States and Kazakhstan had now become sufficiently close for us to carry out such sensitive operations together.

CHAPTER ELEVEN

THE COUNTRY WHERE DREAMS COME TRUE

O N 29 July, 1991, when President Bush visited Moscow, I was invited by Mikhail Gorbachev to become a member of the official Soviet delegation. It was only when we met that I discovered the real reason: oil. For three years, the Soviet government had been negotiating with Chevron, the American oil giant, over joint development of the massive Tengiz field, which lies off the coast of Kazakhstan. Progress had been slow. In the American system, the country's political leaders are not normally directly involved in business deals being pursued by their companies, but this was more than just a normal piece of business. The sheer size of the reserves to be exploited made the deal far larger than anything else ever attempted by a Western company with the Soviet Union; some people were even calling it the 'deal of the century'.

Bush wanted to know how the deal was going and why negotiations seemed to have been dragging on for so long. It did not take me long to explain the problem. Chevron wanted a 30 per cent share of the proceeds for themselves, well above the usual international norms. We were eventually able to persuade them to modify their demands, but that was still several years down the line.

Soviet, and especially Kazakh, oil specialists had been aware for decades of both the size and the potential of the oil and gas resources on the territory of the Caspian depression, particularly in the district of Southern Emba. However, although the first surveys were carried out during the 1930s, it was not until the 1970s that knowledge and technology were sufficiently advanced to allow real results. Even then, the government in Moscow was chiefly concerned with developing the vast oil reserves of western Siberia and did not devote much attention to the Caspian.

The task of developing the field fell to Embaoil, one of the oldest oil enterprises in Kazakhstan, whose specialists studied all the data in great detail and in 1971 came up with detailed proposals, which they presented to the Soviet ministry of oil production. Finally, after going from office to office in Moscow and getting all the various agreements which were typically necessary in that period, they obtained permission to begin exploration. The Kazakh specialists did the best they could with the resources and equipment at their disposal and soon came up with results: by 1976 they had located 30 potential drilling sites and were given the go-ahead to start developing them.

The first test boring in 1979 gave a fantastic result – some 475 cubic metres of oil per day. When I heard about it I was reminded of a cartoon in an old newspaper of an

American dentist drilling a hole in an Arab sheikh's tooth and watching oil come flowing out of it. Suddenly, western Kazakhstan, one of the poorest, most god-forsaken places on earth, looked, like much of the Arab world, as if it could turn into a kind of Klondike.

Before being sure, though, it was necessary to carry out more extensive exploration. A group of experts was set up and given the best equipment available in the Soviet Union. This would allow them not only to determine the precise character of the oil, gas and other components, but also to come up with an idea of the potential value of the field. A state commission, which was handling all their data, finally came to its conclusion in 1986: the total reserves of oil reached 2.648 billion tonnes. This was the beginning of Tengiz.

However, from the beginning there were enormous problems. Although the Soviet Union was the world's largest producer and exporter of oil, accounting for one fifth of world-wide production, the peculiar nature of its command economy meant that the money earned ended up in the state budget rather than being ploughed back into the oil industry. There were just not enough resources to fully develop such a large field. In addition, there were enormous technical problems: the oil was extremely sour and corrosive and was lying beneath salt domes at extraordinarily high temperature and pressure. Soviet industry was unable to make the high quality pipes need to handle it. In 1995, one well had burst open and stayed on fire for a year, sending flames climbing 100 metres into the air. There was a danger that the same thing would happen again. Hurtful as it was to national pride, it was clear that the Soviet Union would not be able to develop the field on its own: it needed expertise that only the West had.

The first idea was to create a consortium. The authorities turned to Armand Hammer, the veteran American entrepreneur, who had been doing business with the Soviet Union since the early days of the Bolshevik revolution. Hammer introduced several different Western oil companies which all made studies of the field's potential. None of them went ahead: the conditions were too difficult and the oil was of too poor quality, and too sulphurous. So the consortium idea died. It was shortly after that the name of Chevron first came up.

Chevron became involved in the Soviet Union in the late 1980s as part of a six-company American trade consortium which was formed in order to look into the possibility of pursuing joint ventures there; Johnson and Johnson, Eastman Kodak and RJR Nabisco were among the others involved. At the time, the Soviet rouble was still not convertible. And so, despite the huge potential for business in the Soviet Union, many Western companies held back from becoming involved because they had no way of converting any profits they made from roubles back into 'hard' – that is Western – currency. Crude oil, one of the few Soviet products which could be sold abroad for dollars, was an obvious solution. The consortium's members began to consider the idea of using the proceeds from the sale of crude oil or oil products from the former

Soviet Union to recoup the investment which the group would make in business which would generate only 'soft' currency.

Chevron had already looked into the possibility of building petrochemical facilities in western Siberia but had rejected the idea. Since then, it was known that they were on the look-out for other projects. They immediately looked like promising partners for us. Their experts convinced our specialists of their experience in working in the Gulf of Mexico. Importantly, they also made clear that they had the necessary technology to respect the sensitive ecological balance of the Caspian Sea. Almost seven decades of Communist rule had turned large parts of Kazakhstan and the rest of the Soviet Union into an ecological wasteland. We were determined not to make things worse.

At first, the Americans were interested not in the Tengiz field, but in the Korolevskoye field a few miles away. After drawing up an appropriate agreement with the then Soviet government, headed by Nikolai Ryzhkov, they began a detailed study in 1989. But the results showed that the field was not really large enough on its own to be of interest to them. So they then turned their attention to the Tengiz field. Once they carried out their studies there, and discovered quite how large that field was, they quickly made clear their interest. Tengiz ranked with some of the largest oil fields in the world.

It was just over a year later, in June 1990, during Gorbachev's trip to America for the Washington Summit, that the first concrete step was taken. On 2 June, a protocol of intent was signed between the two sides giving Chevron exclusive rights to explore and develop the Tengiz oil field.

The deal caused enormous excitement. It was the largest-newly discovered oil field, spanning 44,200 hectares. Although not all of the oil was necessarily recoverable, it was estimated that it would yield some 25 billion barrels of oil – or two and a half times as much oil as Prudhoe Bay in Alaska. There had been some nervousness about allowing a foreign company to become involved in developing such a large field, but by then it was clear that there was little alternative. In the spring of 1990, one Soviet newspaper, *Rabochaya Tribuna*, estimated that delays in developing Tengiz had already cost the country more than 20 million barrels in lost production of crude oil, as well as large volumes of gas, sulphur, ethane and propane. It had long been a question not of whether we would co-operate with Chevron, but on which terms.

At the end of July, just over a month after Gorbachev's visit, I, too, went to America. In my function as a Minister and then as Prime Minister, I had already travelled widely abroad as part of Soviet delegations, including to the United States, but this visit stood out for me because of its intensity and because of the impressions I gathered.

One of the main tasks of my trip was to drum up interest in Kazakhstan. I certainly made an impact. 'Like a one man chamber of commerce, the President of Kazakhstan, the second largest republic in the Soviet Union, is trying to convince Americans that his mineral-rich region would be a good place to do business,' wrote the *New York Times*.

James Giffin, the President of the American trade consortium, had set up an intense programme of meeting and contacts for my visit, including key political and business leaders. I recall in particular a meeting at the New York Committee of International Relations, a prestigious organisation which brought together leading politicians, including even some former Presidents. There was lively discussion about urgent international problems. Most importantly, we all agreed that economic reforms within the former Soviet Union were a vital step towards improving relations with the rest of the world.

The interest was tempered with caution. During my visit, Nicholas Brady, the Treasury secretary, warned of the difficulties which Western companies faced in making a profit in the Soviet Union, pointing out that many US businessmen were still unwilling to go there. There was the further problem that the Soviet Union was already behind on US $2–4 billion worth of payments of its existing foreign debt. Some dozen American companies were so alarmed at what was happening that they got together to ask the Commerce Department to intercede on their behalf. I was not afraid to discuss this problem openly. 'I think the Soviet government has been going about this all wrong,' I told journalists at one meeting. 'It should not be frightening off the foreign businessmen with whom they should be dealing.'

I also tried to make it clear that Kazakhstan was in a completely different situation from Lithuania, which had declared its sovereignty earlier that year and immediately faced a Kremlin blockade. Our aim, I told the Americans, was economic sovereignty rather than political separatism, with the aim of developing the republic's wealth for the benefit of the local people. Indeed, a first important step had already been taken in that direction, thanks to the passing of a law which gave the individual Soviet republics effective control of natural resources on their territory.

Much of my time was taken up by detailed talks with Chevron at their headquarters in San Francisco. It was there that I met the company's chief executive Kenneth Derr and other senior members of management for the first time.

Derr was clearly unhappy about the way negotiations with the Soviet authorities were going. 'Moscow is just dragging its feet,' he complained. 'An incredible amount of time is spent on discussing the smallest details, but all the major decisions are always being postponed.'

I could not answer for Moscow, but was ready to give my own opinion.

'If you want to solve the problems quickly, then you should not bother trying to discuss things with Moscow at all,' I said. 'You should deal with us directly.'

Then, when we had finished discussing all the technical problems, I surprised my hosts by shifting the discussion away from oil and asking them what the company was planning to do for the Tengiz region as a whole. As far as I was concerned, it was a vital part of the project. During the Soviet years, the authorities had devoted far too little attention to the well-being of the people and to their social and cultural life. The main priority was always production. Everything else was secondary. Why should the people of Tengiz, literally with gold under their feet, continue to live in such terrible conditions? Richard Matzke, the President of Chevron Overseas Petroleum had to admit that the company had given little thought to the social aspects of such a project. Given my insistence he said, Chevron was ready to come to the region to study the social problem.

I was also keen to hear what my hosts had to say about the ecological situation and to learn which steps they planned to take to protect the very delicate flora and fauna from the effects of the exploitation of the oil fields. This time, it was my turn to be surprised. In order to dispel our concerns, Chevron organised a helicopter flight over the Gulf of Mexico where the company had long been drilling for oil. From the cabin of the helicopter, we could see dozens of ships catching fish and prawns around the platforms; the water even right next to the rigs was crystal clear.

An hour later, we visited the oil processing plant on the shore. I was struck by how clean everything was. The area around the installation was strewn with snow-white mussels on which not one drop of oil was visible. I saw wild ducks swimming on the surface of one of the precipitation tanks, herons were circling over another. The water which was being discharged back into the Gulf of Mexico looked perfectly clean.

There was no doubt about my enthusiasm for what I saw at Chevron. However, we were still some way from finalising the deal.

Talks continued on various levels throughout the rest of 1990 and seemed to be going well; the Americans were even optimistic enough to talk about starting to pump oil from 1991. That September, Gorbachev and I met an American trade delegation. Gorbachev was very supportive. We continued to talk about drafting documents to set up the joint venture. In an important reflection of the shift of power to the republics throughout the Soviet Union, it was decided to register the joint venture in Almaty, rather than in Moscow as had been originally planned. Then, on 11 December, 1990, at an official press conference in Moscow, I was finally able to announce that a joint venture was being set up. There was no doubting the scale of the project: the field was the largest discovered in the world in the course of the previous decade and the joint venture was the largest US-Soviet deal in history. But still the terms were not clear. The Americans wanted too large a share of the proceeds.

Increasingly, too, the Tengiz venture was becoming a political football between opposing forces grappling for economic control. However significant the decision to register in Almaty, the Soviet authorities were determined not to share with Kazakhstan that part of the proceeds to which we were rightfully entitled. Those in Moscow did not – or maybe could not – understand that once people have tasted freedom they do not want to be pushed back under the yoke of totalitarianism. For this reason, their relations with us were forever tainted with the remnants of the old colonial policies.

However, I was equally determined to push the deal through – and considered I had the right to do so. I also knew that, with every month that passed, the position of Gorbachev and of the Union authorities was getting weaker, and ours was getting stronger.

There were other more specific hurdles. The first was the Russian presidential elections of June 1991 in which Ryzhkov, who had become identified with the Tengiz deal during his time as Prime Minister, was the main opponent of Boris Yeltsin. Opponents of Ryzhkov openly attacked the terms under discussion as too favourable to Chevron and demanded a change. In May, an article in the newspaper, *Moscow News*, put their position: under the headline 'How to turn a huge field into a black hole with no profit'. It criticised the deal as a sell-out of Soviet natural resources. The attack was quickly taken up by other Soviet newspapers, even those pro-market ones which were normally in favour of co-operation with the West. There was no doubt that officials within Gosplan, the Soviet state planning agency, were trying to stir up trouble as part of their struggle to avoid ceding economic powers to the individual republics.

The row eventually calmed down. Then, in August, came the failed *coup*, followed by the break-up of the Soviet Union at the end of the year. It was virtually impossible to make progress on such a large deal at a time of such political turbulence.

Ultimately, independence made it far easier for us to find a solution. Not only had Gosplan gone, but the whole Soviet level of government with it. It was now up to the Kazakh government alone to negotiate with Chevron. So, in May 1992, shortly before my visit to the United States, I signed a protocol with Chevron Overseas Petroleum Inc. setting up a joint venture for a 40-year work programme to develop the Tengiz deposits. The joint venture, named Tengizchevroil, was between the Chevron Overseas Company and the Kazakh production association, Tengizneftegaz. I formally signed the deal with Kenneth Derr, Chevron's Chairman and CEO, on 19 May, hours after I arrived in Washington on an official visit which was otherwise dominated by my talks on arms control with President Bush.

It was a huge step forward, but the devil was in the details, many of which had still to be decided. It was not just a matter of the precise share of profits between the two partners; there were also a wide range of other legal and tax-related matters which had to be hammered out between the two sides. Chevron obviously wanted the best terms for themselves – but then, so did we. In addition, the whole negotiation process was slowed by the replacement in July 1992 of one of the Kazakh Vice-Premiers who had been involved in all the preparatory work for the contract.

By the spring of 1993, I decided that the negotiations had dragged on for too long – it was time for a decision. So in April I sent Chevron a telegram. In it, I proposed that Chevron should receive 19 per cent of the overall profit, rather than 29 per cent as they had originally proposed, and that we should take the remaining 81 per cent. 'If you don't accept within one week then the whole deal is off,' I told them.

My tactics worked. A few days later, Matzke, who was still leading the negotiations for Chevron, arrived in Almaty with a letter finally accepting the conditions. Then, on 6 April, the memorandum to create the 40-year project and a number of other documents were finally signed at a formal ceremony. The mood was exuberant. One Chevron manager could barely contain his emotion, shouting out 'We finally did it!' after both sides had put their signatures to the documents. A five-year long courtship had at last culminated in marriage.

The deal formally created Tengizchevroil, a 50/50 joint venture between Chevron Overseas Petroleum Inc., Chevron's international exploration and production subsidiary, and Tengizneftegaz, a subsidiary of Kazakhstan's national oil company. Under the terms of the agreement, the partners would invest $20 billion over 40 years to exploit the Tengiz and Korolovsky fields. As part of this, Chevron pledged to open an account for US$700 million immediately, out of which it would not only cover development costs, but also pay bonuses to the Kazakh government and transfer US$10 million a year to the Atyrausky region on whose territory the field lay.

With estimated reserves of 6–20 billion barrels of oil, the field was reportedly twice as big as Alaska's Prudhoe Bay field. For Chevron, it was their biggest international contract since the early 1970s. Tengizchevroil was also the biggest joint venture enterprise in the whole CIS.

It had taken us just under a year, from the signature of the first protocol, to the conclusion of the agreement. Given the novelty and the magnitude of the project, it was not very long. Other contracts on such a scale have often taken years to conclude. Of course, we did not get it all our own way, but then neither did Chevron. As Derr remarked after the signing: 'If I were 100 per cent happy with all the details, President Nazarbayev wouldn't be sitting here with me today.'

It was as much a political as an economic event, which had significance not just for Kazakhstan, but also for the entire former Soviet Union. That a Western company had decided to conclude such a deal with us, on purely commercial grounds, showed to the world the seriousness of Kazakhstan's intentions to work with the world business community. In October 1996, on Kazakhstan's National Day, Derr sent me a congratulatory telegram in which he pointed out how well our venture was going. I agreed with him. The successful outcome of this project has sharply raised the level of confidence in Kazakhstan and greatly helped the country's image abroad.

From the beginning, the key question for Kazakhstan has been how to transport the oil extracted from the Tengiz field to customers abroad. It is also an issue which has been closely linked to our relations with Russia. This was confirmed immediately after we had signed the deal to create Tengizchevroil. In direct contravention of an earlier agreement, the Russians, citing ecological concerns, began to oppose the transport of large amounts of oil through their territory. As a result, we were obliged to cut the amount of oil extracted from the Tengiz field by more than half – to some 65,000 barrels a day.

It is difficult to avoid the impression that there are some influential people in Moscow who, to put it mildly, are not interested in the success of our Tengiz operation. Claims that Russia does not have enough pipeline capacity to export its own oil are hardly convincing. It seems instead that Russia is determined to have control over the access which Kazakhstan enjoys to the Western market.

The main solution to this problem remains the project for the Caspian Pipeline Consortium (KTK), which, beside Kazakhstan, includes Russia and the Sultanate of Oman. The pipeline runs from the Tengiz field through Russian territory to the Russian port of Novorossiisk. The original agreement ensured that the pipeline would be financed by the Sultanate of Oman. Unfortunately, Oman had not fulfilled its commitment by the contract date of 1 October, 1995 – and this remained the sole problem preventing us from starting work.

The problem was as follows: since Tengizchevroil was to be the main user of this pipeline, the Caspian Pipeline Consortium asked Chevron for a guarantee that it would use the pipeline to transport its oil, offering the company in return 'b' class, non-voting shares in the project. Chevron did not accept this proposal; nor did it accept the proposed tariffs.

Whatever the head of the consortium thought, even if Chevron *had* offered these guarantees, they would not have constituted a sufficient basis on which to receive credit from the international financial institutions.

In order to solve the problem, we started to look for other partners. Logically, the first place to start was with those oil companies which were already working successfully in Kazakhstan. Our initial discussions showed that this was the right approach. When we spoke to senior bankers from the World Bank and the European Bank for Reconstruction and Development, who have considerable experience of the financing of such projects, they also agreed with us.

The attitude of Russia remained crucial. For that reason, I invited Viktor Chernomyrdin, the Russian Prime Minister, to visit the city of Uralsk in western Kazakhstan in October 1995, so that he could take a look at the situation for himself. Our main topic of conversation was how our two countries together could best develop our resources of oil and gas. Then, the following month, I went to Moscow to visit President Yeltsin, who at that time was undergoing a course of treatment in the Kremlin clinic. As well as wishing Yeltsin well, I wanted to discuss a few matters of mutual interest to our two countries. They all concerned oil: the problem of the creation of KTK; the development and exploitation of the Karachaganak gas condensate field; the development of the resources of the Caspian and the use of the Russian transport network to carry our oil.

Because of his poor health, I only briefly mentioned these matters. However, defying the advice of his doctors, Yeltsin insisted on having formal talks and wanted to know all the details. Our discussions went extremely well and we agreed that Russian companies should play as important a role as Western ones both in developing the fields and in transporting the oil. This ensured that Russia would have a direct interest in the success of the whole project.

On the basis of our study of the problem, and of the discussions which we held with the Russian leadership, I drew up a list of 10 principles which was circulated to those involved in the project. According to these principles, all those taking part – namely Chevron, Agip, British Gas, Oriks, Lukoil, Rosneft, Shell and Munaygas – were obliged to provide funds and financial guarantees for the realisation of the project in return for which they would together receive a 50 per cent share of the pipeline. The remaining 50 per cent would remain in the hands of the founding members of KTK – Kazakhstan, Russia and the Sultanate of Oman.

The effort which we have put into ensuring the success of this project has convinced us that Kazakhstan's need to transport oil to the export markets of the West will increase every year. For that reason, we have continued to examine various options. One possibility is to try to increase the amount of oil which we are able to transport along existing Russian pipelines in return for investing appropriate amounts in its reconstruction and modernisation. We are also looking at the feasibility of transporting our oil away to the South through Iran, Turkey and the Mediterranean. The fact that Azerbaijan has begun carrying out major oil projects in the Caspian has also made the ultimate success of this project more likely.

Separately, the Japanese government, together with some major companies, has come up with the idea of building an oil and gas pipeline from Turkmenistan through Kazakhstan and China out to the Pacific coast opposite China. This is obviously some way in the future, but is also potentially of great interest.

In 1979, on the territory of western Kazakhstan, local geologists opened up a massive field of gas and condensate which proved to be the second largest in the world. It was named after the nearby village of Karachaganak.

A few years later, a delegation of senior officials from several federal ministries and agencies visited Uralsk. Much attention was paid to a speech by Nikolai Baibakov, Chairman of Gosplan, the state planning agency. He said that Karachaganak would become a powerful catalyst for the social and economic development of the region. Later, Nikolai Ryzhkov, the Soviet Prime Minister, also came to see what was being described as the 'Kazakh wonder'. I remember a meeting there which I attended in my capacity as Prime Minister of Kazakhstan. 'Soon an important document about Karachaganak will be adopted,' Ryzhkov said, 'but let us be patient and wait a little.'

Finally, in 1985, a special joint resolution of the Central Committee of the Soviet Communist Party and of the Council of Ministers was adopted on the development and equipping of the Karachaganak field. The proposals took one's breath away. As well as developing the field itself, considerable attention was paid to tackling the region's most pressing social and environmental problems. By 1991, the field was to be pumping out up to 15 million tonnes of condensate and oil a year and 20 to 26 billion cubic metres of gas. Importantly, it was proposed to build a gas processing plant right next to the field, ensuring that Kazakhstan drew the full benefit from its resources rather than merely being used as a source of raw materials. Some 300 to 350 million roubles were to be invested in the project, which was an enormous sum for that period. As part of the plan, Aksai, the little village in the centre of the field with a population of 11,000, was to turn into a major town of 120,000 people. Since everything was planned on a grand scale, it was even decided to bring in 4,000 construction workers from East Germany, Czechoslovakia and Bulgaria, who were used to working to a far higher standard than their Russian counterparts.

Unfortunately, everything turned out very differently. In 1987, Moscow issued another government resolution which put a dampener on our enthusiasm. Although ordering a doubling of output, it also announced that plans to develop industry around the field had been dropped. Instead of being processed on the spot, the gas and oil would be piped across the border and sent for processing in the Russian cities of Orenburg, Ufa and Salavat. This meant that those cities would receive much of the money which it had originally been intended to spend on developing the social infrastructure around the field. The decision came as an enormous shock, but we knew that there was nothing that we could do about it. Once again, Kazakhstan would be left merely supplying raw materials to Russia, which had reaffirmed its determination not to allow its 'little brother' to become too big for its boots.

Morale in Karachaganak plunged and some of the local workers went on strike, which was virtually unimaginable in those days. The authorities, meanwhile, completely forgot about their promises to protect the environment and there were major gas leaks. Such was the damage done that the local parliament even adopted a resolution to stop the exploitation of the field. Some of the discontent was open, some of it hidden, but the tension in the area was palpable. It reminded me of the situation in the steelworks at Temirtau just before the uprising in 1959 and I was worried that the situation might repeat itself here.

Developing this unique and technically complicated field required enormous investment; money which, as usual, was neither in the budget of the ministry nor of the federal government. The only real solution would have been foreign investors. But, at that time, the Soviet government was in no hurry to seek help from the West and the authorities in Almaty were still firmly bound by what was decided in Moscow.

It was only as the Soviet Union was beginning to crumble that the Kazakh government was free enough to take the initiative to remedy the situation. In October 1990, the republic's Committee for Foreign Economic Relations signed an initial protocol of intention with British Gas to develop the field jointly. At the same time, several other companies, such as British Petroleum, and Agip (part of Italy's ENI group), began to show interest in Karachaganak.

However, there were still problems: the Soviet Union still formally existed and the authorities in Moscow did not raise a finger to create the legal or economic framework making it possible to draw up contracts with foreign companies. Even so, Kazakhstan decided to take the risk and created a new gas company, Kazakhgazprom, based on the reserves in the field and the network of pipelines on our territory. Surprisingly, the Soviet authorities did not actively object, partly because I had already smoothed the path by meeting Viktor Chernomyrdin, who had not yet become Russian Prime Minister and was at that time head of Gazprom, the powerful Russian gas company.

For the first time in Soviet history, we organised a competitive tender among foreign investors to decide who would have the right to develop the field. It was no easy task to do something like that from scratch, particularly since no one in the Kazakh government had been involved in such a project before. However, to the great credit of our Kazakh experts we were able to prepare all the necessary documentation very quickly and in March 1992, we announced the tender. Three months later, in June, we signed a protocol on exploiting Karachaganak with the winners, an alliance of British Gas and Agip. The losing alliance of British Petroleum and Norway's Statoil took defeat with good grace.

In the five years since then, the project has begun to work, although it would be wrong to say that everything has gone smoothly. The development could have been faster. However, the one problem which prevents foreign companies from investing more in the field are the very high fees, levied by the Russian oil and gas industry, on processing and transport.

Although our decision to put the field under Kazakh jurisdiction generated much more revenue for the republic, the fact that the processing was still being carried out in Russia meant that some 70 per cent of the proceeds from the gas condensate and 50 per cent from the gas ended up in the hands of the plants in Orenburg, Ufa and Salavat. When Kazakhstan became independent in 1991, securing some of this 'added value' for ourselves became a reality. We therefore supported the proposal of British Gas and Agip to change the scheme of development of the field and return to the original plan under which processing plants would be set up on the field and a series of pipelines built to transport the finished product to users both at home and abroad.

Kazakhstan is fortunate in having enormous reserves of oil and gas offshore in the Kazakh sector of the Caspian Sea. The search for oil there is of vital importance to the republic, but again it is very difficult for Kazakhstan to do on its own, as we lack the necessary specialists and expertise. So we decided to create another international consortium to carry out a geological and geophysical study of the Kazakh part of the

Caspian Sea. The consortium, Kazakhstankaspishelf, created in 1993, brought together Agip, British Gas, the British Petroleum-Statoil alliance, Mobil, Total of France and Anglo-Dutch Shell. All the companies have experience of working in conditions similar to those on the Caspian Shelf and also have good records on protecting the environment.

The consortium's overall budget for the exploration phase amounted to US$280 million. Its members were required to make a non-refundable contribution of US$75 million to the Kazakh state budget. Given the considerable investment which the consortium has made in the project and the risk which it is bearing, its members have been given certain guarantees.

In May 1996, I paid a visit to the region and was impressed by how business-like the people working there were and how good morale was. I was struck by how almost all of our specialists were quite at home speaking English with their foreign partners. It reminded me of my trip to see Chevron's rigs in the Gulf of Mexico where I had seen so many different nationalities working side by side. Another positive thing about the project was the effort which the consortium was putting into developing the social infra-structure in the nearby regions of Atyrau and Mangistau. Although no oil had yet begun to flow, the local people were already beginning to feel its positive effects.

The success of the venture made me wonder whether the same model could not be applied in the Aral Sea and the surrounding region. This region, best known for its chronic environmental problems, is also believed to have substantial oil and gas deposits, even though they are smaller than those in the Caspian, and several Western companies have already expressed interest. Why not make use of some of the money which would pour in for exploration there to begin to clean up the environment as well?

The development of the Caspian Sea has not been without problems, most notably concerning the legal status of the sea itself. The legal regime governing the Caspian Sea centres on treaties which the Soviet Union and Iran signed in 1921 and 1940. However, these cover only fishing and navigation rights and not the Sea's legal status in the fullest sense of the term. The break-up of the Soviet Union and the emergence around the Caspian of four new states – Kazakhstan, Russia, Azerbaijan and Turkmenistan – alongside Iran added a further complication. It therefore became necessary to draw up a more comprehensive agreement which would allow us to demarcate areas such as shipping, fishing, the development of mineral reserves and ecology.

The Kazakh position is that we should divide up all the reserves which lie beneath the Caspian between the various states. As far as fish stocks, shipping rights and other issues are concerned, we are prepared for any kind of compromise.

Essentially, we are looking for mutual understanding with all countries. In April 1996, during President Yeltsin's visit to Almaty, a joint Kazakh-Russian declaration was signed on the use of the Caspian Sea. I signed a similar agreement in May of the same year in Teheran with President Rafsanjani, the Iranian President, and in September, in Baku, with Geidar Aliyev, the Azerbaijan President. Then, in November 1996, the foreign ministers of the countries which border the Caspian gathered at a summit to discuss the outstanding questions. Unfortunately, they did not manage to reach total agreement, but there is no doubt that an arrangement which is acceptable to all will eventually be reached. In the meantime, though, Kazakhstan has confined itself to working only in the Gulf of the Caspian which clearly lies within the republic's territory.

Over the next decade, Kazakhstan has the opportunity of becoming one of the main exporters of hydrocarbon fuels in the world. However, this is not a goal in itself. Our main task is to make use of the development of the oil and gas sector to ensure the balanced development of the economy as a whole.

The oil and gas industry, like other sectors of the economy, require enormous investment. This has meant attracting foreign investors. In order to achieve this we have had to create a favourable investment climate. Concretely, this means that Kazakhstan has been ready to establish a system of serious preferences which would help the development of the domestic market and, at the same time, create good conditions for foreign investors, especially in sectors which are a priority for the government's development plans.

The development of infra-structure is especially important: the Transasian railways, already mentioned, are an important part of this; so is the agreement which we signed with the European Bank for Reconstruction and Development to rebuild the Caspian Sea port of Aktau and the decision to open up new air routes linking Kazakhstan with a number of other countries.

We have also concluded agreements with the World Bank to develop a number of programmes. One of them involves the setting up of a modern system of registration of land and property. This, in turn, will help provide the pre-conditions which we need to develop a genuine property market and bring it up to world standards. Considerable assistance has been received from the Asian Development Bank, whose credits we have used for improving our infra-structure and modernising our agriculture. These measures have allowed Kazakhstan to make use of its national riches and help speed up the further transformation of the economy. Even the most cautious of foreign businessmen are now convinced that the pre-conditions are there to ensure that Kazakhstan is a stable place where it is possible to plan for long-term projects.

Given sufficient investment, our country has the chance to become one of the leading exporters of oil, equipment, ferrous and non-ferrous metal and food products. The chemical industry, and the fertiliser sector in particular, is especially interesting to foreign investors. Other sectors which would benefit from foreign investment include the pipeline and power-generating industries. The food processing industry is another promising area: every year, 20 to 22 million tonnes of wheat are harvested in Kazakhstan and, on the basis of that, we have a substantial stock breeding industry. However, a considerable amount of money must be put in to develop it.

Finally, there are major possibilities in the field of high technology, including a number of former defence plants, which we are in the process of privatising. The level of technology is often very high; after all, one of the plants used to produce SS-20 missiles.

So far, Kazakhstan has received around US$50 billion worth of investment, from the United States, Britain and several other European countries, and from Asia. However, we need yet more if we are going to continue the process of developing and modernising our country.

CHAPTER TWELVE

THE IMPERATIVE OF THE NEXT CENTURY

Today nobody has any doubts that Kazakhstan is established as an independent state and a fully-fledged member of the world community. This has not happened by chance. It has been a direct result of the foreign policy which we have pursued. It was clear to us from the beginning that without international recognition of our state, and international guarantees of our borders and of the integrity of our territory, our assertion of sovereignty and our economic reforms would come to nothing. It was essential for us to be able to integrate into the world community. This, in turn, would come only after we had proved that Kazakhstan was able to make a worthy contribution to the new world order.

I remember when we were getting ready recently to celebrate the 50th anniversary of the end of World War II. As part of my preparations for the traditional meeting with war veterans, I asked my aides to collect together some material from the film archives of the war and the immediate post-war years. These old frames took me back half a century, evoking again the overwhelming feeling of victory which we had at the time. Red Square in Moscow, the streets around the White House in Washington, Times Square in New York, the boulevards of Paris and the square in front of Whitehall and Buckingham Palace in London – even though the footage was in black and white, it clearly showed the colour of joy on the people's faces. As I looked at it, I could not help thinking how alike people are the world over.

They were alike, not only because they had been fighting side by side, but also because they were united in their desire to build a new world – one without violence and hostility, a world in which nations and peoples work together with each other. The United Nations was set up precisely in order to help create such a world.

Unfortunately, that generation's dream did not become reality. The former allies divided the world between themselves and began another war – the Cold War. As the two sides traded accusations and insults, a massive arms race got underway and intensified as the years passed. Entire continents became caught up in the battle for the spheres of influence; at any moment the entire world was in danger of being destroyed through an exchange of nuclear weapons.

Now, as we stand on the threshold of the twenty-first century, we are presented with the same question that the previous generation faced 50 years ago: what sort of world should we be trying to create? Only now do we have a chance of trying to realise their dream of ensuring peace through the creation of a united family of nations and peoples.

In considering this, it is important to note one highly important circumstance: the war in Europe ended more than 50 years ago, but it has still not ended for the countries of the former Soviet bloc; it did not end when the last Soviet troops left Poland, Hungary and the other countries of Central and Eastern Europe, not even when they at last won full independence. Neither the East nor the West (which, after all, bear joint responsibility for the Cold War) have yet apologised to the people for what they did. It is unimportant now who takes the first step; the important thing is to set a precedent.

The Soviet Union itself has disappeared from the map and so, strictly speaking, there is no one from whom one could demand such an apology, but there are the 'post-Soviet' states, the former Soviet republics. I believe that the world is still waiting for an apology from them. For this reason, I took advantage of the celebrations marking the 50th anniversary both of the end of World War II and of the creation of the United Nations Organisation, to express formal regret on behalf of Kazakhstan for its part in the moral and physical harm which was caused by the Cold War and to extend the hand of friendship to all countries which were ready to engage in honest and open dialogue. I also promised that my country would do everything to resist any attempt to return to the totalitarian past and to ensure that the world did not again suffer war, whether 'hot' or 'cold'.

Now that the main principles of Kazakhstan's foreign policy have been laid down, we can concentrate on the concrete details of relations with our foreign partners. Our country, situated as it is between Europe and Asia, lies between several influential geopolitical blocs: China, Russia and the Muslim world, in which I also include the countries within the Central Asian union. This has greatly determined the content of Kazakhstan's foreign policy, and will continue to do so. It has also given us a particular strategic advantage, the realisation of which will make it possible not only to develop our country but also to help develop a climate of co-operation and trust on the European continent and ultimately in the world.

One of our main strategic priorities has been to encourage the further integration of the members of the CIS on a number of levels, both multilateral and bilateral. This means, in particular, co-operation in the economic sphere, especially in policy relating to the exploitation of energy and water resources, the environment, the construction and use of oil and gas pipelines and the building of transport links.

Kazakhstan's relations with China have also reached a new, high level, thanks to a number of bilateral meetings which have taken place both in Beijing and Almaty. The treaty which I signed with Tsiang Tse-Min, the leader of the People's Republic of China, is of a long-term character and will greatly improve relations between our two countries. Kazakhstan is the only one of the Central Asian States to have such an agreement with China. This strengthening of bilateral relations corresponds to the long-term interests of both our countries, especially since China appears poised, together with some of the other countries of the Asian-Pacific region, to play an increasingly important role in the first decades of the next century.

The improvement in relations between our two countries greatly helps the maintenance of peace and stability in Asia. In this context, the agreement which we signed in 1994 on regulating border questions with China is especially important for Kazakhstan. This was followed by the unprecedented five-nation agreement signed in April 1996 in Shanghai by Kazakhstan, China, Russia, Tajikistan and Kyrgyzstan on confidence-building measures in the military sphere in the border areas. This sharply increases the chance of maintaining stability across a huge geographical area and strengthens the security of all our countries.

A stable long-term strategic interest for us is also represented by the European Union, relations with which have assumed a more dynamic and practical character over the last few years. This was symbolised by the agreement on partnership and co-operation which we signed with the EU at the beginning of 1995.

Kazakhstan's links with Germany have been developing well: the German government and, in particular, Helmut Kohl, whom I have met on many occasions, is very understanding of our problems, especially with respect to the specific questions posed by the existence of the large German community which lives on our territory.

Kohl, both as a politician and as person, is such a colourful, larger-than-life figure that it would be a shame not to digress a little to talk about him. Like all politicians, he was once young and inexperienced, but it is difficult to imagine that when one deals with him now. For me, he is the face of modern Germany, both strong and powerful. Such an experienced politician as Kohl has good reason to consider himself as a kind of patriarch; he was the one who united Germany and brought it to its current powerful position in the world. When he became Chancellor in 1982, he was the youngest person ever to occupy the post. Christened by journalists the 'Fox of the Rhine', he has made a point of pursuing a policy of openness. This may be largely image, but it is certainly a successful one, and, in politics, image is all-important. Kohl is standing for re-election in autumn 1998 and I hope that he wins: it is too early for such a figure to leave political life.

Our relationship with France is extremely important, especially with regard to increasing Kazakhstan's prominence on the international stage, and in particular, within the EU. François Mitterrand, the late President, did much to further relations between our two countries. I always liked him for his personal charm and modesty and admired him not just as a politician, but also as a successful literary figure, who published 14 books. Such simplicity (in the positive sense of the word) and openness characterised many of the real heroes of France, especially those like Mitterrand, whom we also admired for the active role which he played in the French resistance during World War II.

Mitterrand was replaced in 1995 by Jacques Chirac, with whom we have also established a positive dialogue. I met Chirac for the first time during my visit to France in

1994, when he was still mayor of Paris. I have always been greatly impressed by the policy of Gaullism, of which Chirac remains a strong exponent, and which has propelled France to such a prominent place in the world. My first impression of our meeting was of his broad, almost Hollywood-type smile, which could not mask his intelligence and mastery of detail. I may be wrong, but his life puts me in mind of that of Boris Yeltsin; both have been full of dramatic peaks and troughs. Like Yeltsin, Chirac finally achieved his goal – namely the supreme post of leader of his country. I am sure that he will continue to use his power for the good of France.

Kazakh-British relations are also good, especially concerning the question of the joint exploitation of Kazakhstan's vast resources of energy: when I met John Major, the former British Prime Minister, we agreed on the need for close co-operation.

We are also trying to re-establish relations with the former Communist countries of Eastern Europe, especially the Baltic States, Hungary, Poland, Bulgaria and the others.

One of our most important foreign partners is the United States. If at first our relations largely centred on the nuclear question and the legacy of the nuclear weapons which we inherited from the Soviet Union, they have since turned into equal co-operation, based on the charter of democratic partnership which we concluded. A whole range of treaties and agreements between us in the trade and economic spheres has begun to operate, most notably an agreement giving us 'most favoured nation' status. Kazakhstan also benefits from the general system of preferences. My relations with Bill Clinton, whether on the basis of meetings, telephone conversations or written messages, are extremely good and go beyond purely bilateral matters. We both share an interest in matters of international security; we have had long conversations about the Tajik-Afghan problem. And I am pleased to say that we agree on many issues.

As I wrote above, I first met Clinton when I visited America in 1994. We got on well with each other from the start. During a reception in the Oval Hall of the White House I gave him several presents, including a carpet decorated with a colourful image of Clinton and his wife, Hillary. Seeing a puzzled look on his face, I explained to him that, according to tradition in Central Asia, carpets are not only laid on the floor, but also hung on the walls as decoration. Clinton nodded in understanding and called in one of his aides to take the carpet away and put it in an 'appropriate place'. Imagine my surprise when I left the room later after our negotiations and saw my gift lying on the floor. Even worse, a secretary was actually standing on the carpet, with the sharp tip of her stiletto heel sticking into Clinton's nose. Seeing my expression, Clinton burst out laughing and rubbed his own nose.

Strange as it may sound, in the light of the recent problems concerning his private life, Clinton had always come across to me as rather a formal person. I remember an incident on the margins of a meeting of world leaders at an OSCE (the Organisation for Security and Co-operation in Europe) summit in Budapest in 1995. Yeltsin motioned to Clinton to come to one side with him, presumably for a confidential discussion, sat down on one of the sofas which were in the hall and gestured to Clinton to do the same. However, Clinton demonstrably declined to do so and remained standing. I could read from his face what he was thinking: why should I sit down if all the other Presidents, apart from you, Mr Yeltsin, are standing? Although the Americans as a people are renowned for not standing on ceremony, Clinton has always keenly observed protocol.

Our relations with Japan and the Republic of Korea have developed well, despite the recent economic crisis in both countries. As part of our policy of developing the Kazakh economy, it has been crucial for us to look at ways of attracting investment and the transfer of technology from these countries. I remember one particular episode, during my visit to Japan in 1994. Our talks with the government had gone extremely well – so well, in fact, that Emperor Hirohito congratulated me on the positive state of Kazakh-Japanese relations. Our negotiations on one of the evenings ended with the signature of a number of agreements which would have the effect of opening wide the door for mutually beneficial co-operation of all sorts. The next day we discovered that the entire government had been forced to resign. It was the first time that something like that had ever happened to me and I was extremely dismayed. However, within one hour of our having received this news, a special courier arrived from the Japanese foreign ministry with a letter assuring us that the change of government did not affect the agreements which we had concluded; as is the Japanese tradition, the new administration would respect them in their entirety. They kept their word, and Japan has since become one of the leading investors in Kazakhstan. This made me think of the member states of the CIS, whose governments are forever changing; it would be an extremely good idea if they followed the Japanese example and also respected the agreements made by their predecessors.

Kazakhstan's relations with the ASEAN (Association of South East Asian Nations) countries, especially Indonesia, Malaysia and Singapore, have also developed well. Their own rapid economic development, which suffered only a partial set-back in the turmoil which hit the region starting in late 1997, has been a good example to us of how best to develop our own economy. My admiration of them was enhanced by the visits which I have paid to the countries to meet their leaders and members of the business community.

One of our most important tasks has also been to build on relations with the countries of the Middle East. It is well-known how rich the region is in political, ethnic and religious disputes and for that reason it is worth devoting considerable time to studying it. After analysing the situation there and meeting a number of its heads of state and government, I came to the conclusion that there is considerable scope there for strengthening economic and political co-operation, and setting up some regional and global system of security.

In considering our relations with all these countries, it is clear that we are fully pursuing the goal of world-wide integration. Such a goal is completely achievable; we simply have to rid ourselves of old-style stereotypes, surmount what is often a lack of mutual understanding and work out a broadly acceptable system of norms not just for co-existence but also for co-operation.

In this connection, it is worth digressing slightly to the period of the early 1990s, in the immediate aftermath of independence, when Kazakhstan was still in the process of working out the priorities of its foreign policy. We announced our intention of attempting to establish equal and friendly relations with all our close – and not so close – neighbours as well as with more far-flung countries. This should have been a clear position, easily understandable by all. Sadly this was not the case, and attempts were made to try to push Kazakhstan into various regional, religious and political ventures. At the first summit of Turkic states in Istanbul, for example, our Turkish colleagues drew up plans, which they expected us to endorse, to create a kind of Pan-Turkic association of states. In the documents it was written that, on the basis of our common historical roots, language and culture, we would all strive towards integration with Turkey. Turgut Özal, the Turkish President, was very upset when I refused to sign such a document. It should have been clear to him that I would not go along with this; having just won its independence, Kazakhstan was certainly not going to give it up again in a hurry.

Turkey is not the only country to have tried this. Many Russian politicians and even some members of the Russian government are often talking about their 'special rights' vis-à-vis the former Soviet republics or of our 'obligation' to co-operate with each other. This is often coupled with talk of preventing Kazakhstan and the states of Central Asia from falling into the sphere of influence of other countries, notably the Islamic ones. We have always rejected this, pointing out that we are determined to develop close relations with *all* countries, but only according to the principles of partnership and equal rights and only where it is a matter of mutual benefit to both sides. In this, I have always been supported by my fellow Central Asian leaders, notably Islam Karimov, the Uzbek President, and Askar Akayev, his Kyrgyz counterpart.

Turgut Özal, being a wise and far-sighted politician, got over his initial disappointment and eventually came to understand and appreciate our position. Unfortunately, he died soon afterwards. Out of respect, we named a street in Almaty after him. Our ties with Turkey have continued to grow ever since, not least due to the good relationship which I have come to enjoy with Suleiman Demirel, his successor.

Our broader foreign policy has been helped by our membership of international organisations such as the United Nations, UNESCO (the United Nations Educational, Scientific and Cultural Organisation), ESCAP (the Economic and Social Commission for Asia and the Pacific), UNDP (the United Nations Development Programme), UNEP (the United Nations Environmental Programme) and WHO (the World Health Organisation). Unlike some of the CIS countries, we also enjoy a good relationship with NATO. In this respect, I believe that the alliance took a major step in the right direction when it decided to establish the 'Partnership for Peace' programme with the former member states of the Warsaw Pact.

We have strengthened our relationship with the OSCE. During its meeting in Lisbon in December 1996, I was the only CIS leader who was asked to preside over one of the plenary sessions. This, alone, attests to the reputation which Kazakhstan has won in helping to resolve current international problems. Building on the experience of the OSCE, Kazakhstan has urged the convening of a special conference in Almaty to discuss confidence-building measures in Asia. This idea, which I presented at the 47th session of the General Assembly of the United Nations, has already begun to move closer to realisation: more than 20 countries are taking part in a working group set up to prepare the meeting. The process of forming a sophisticated regional mechanism for preventative diplomacy requires considerable time and effort; slowly but surely, we are moving towards it.

As we near the twenty-first century, it is clear that no international structure can effectively solve all the problems of global security, social-economic development and integration if it does not take into account the new geo-economic balance which is already appearing with the formation of new centres of power in Western Europe, South-East Asia and North America. The most important thing today is to create global and regional security systems which work alongside one another. International security systems must be constructed in such a way that they work not only from the top downwards but also from the bottom upwards. We, in Central Asia, are critically aware of the need to start to strengthen this on a regional basis. This explains not only our desire to organise the Almaty conference but also our active work in the OEC (Organisation of Economic Co-operation) and my speeches at the Islamic Conference.

This being said, many of the problems in our region are of global significance. This includes, in particular, the transport of oil and gas, which is in the interest of the world community, the struggle against drug trafficking, clearing up damage to the environment and so on: in helping to tackle them we will be helping to create the pre-conditions for the political and socio-economic transformation of our own country.

There is a Biblical quotation according to which there is a time to scatter stones and a time to pick them up. There could not be a more appropriate way of describing the situation since the break-up of the Soviet Union in 1991. In the aftermath of the abortive *coup* of August 1991, so many of those stones were thrown to the furthest corners of the Soviet Union that there were more than enough of them to build impregnable walls around all the borders of the newly-independent states. Nobody at the time appeared to worry about the effect of these stone walls on the people, separating national groups and even members of the same families from one another and all but cutting off the oxygen which the once-united economic organism needed in order to function. All this was dismissed as an unimportant and unavoidable side-effect of the broader processes at work.

As the initial euphoria passed, concern grew about the future of the CIS. Everyone seemed worried: workers and businessmen, pensioners and housewives. Every day, when I sat down to read the letters which were sent to the presidential office, I became more and more convinced that people were concerned not just about their own material well-being, but also about the apparent tension in relations between our governments. These letters did not only come from the towns and villages of Kazakhstan; I received some from the furthest corners of the former Soviet Union. I remember one very long letter which I received from Minsk. Pyotr Mokhov, Semyon Chekholski and Timofie Kolyshkin, three veterans of the partisan movement in Belarus during World War II, wrote urging me to do everything in my power to bring the former Soviet republics and their peoples back closer together again. 'You are well-known as a consistent internationalist,' they wrote. 'For that reason, we expect you to come up with a real programme of integration. If Moscow remains silent, then Minsk and Kiev will do the same, but this should not stop Almaty from having its say!'

It was a simple and unsophisticated letter, which made no mention of the international situation in general, but those three veterans hit the nail on the head. They expressed exactly what millions of people were thinking. The world is becoming more and more closely integrated as countries strive to regulate their relations with their neighbours and with countries further afield. There are many such examples: the European Union, the League of Arab States and the inter-governmental associations of Latin America and of the Asia-Pacific region. All these organisations were created with the goal of developing and deepening relations between countries and solving common economic and political problems. It is no longer possible for any country to pursue economic isolationism. Market reform everywhere tends to follow a similar pattern; to ignore this is to resort to a misguided romanticism.

Given its enormous size and relative economic weight, Russia should have been the driving force behind this process of reintegration. Instead, it remained silent for a long time, leaving Kazakhstan to lead the way. Working out a project for a new intergovernmental structure took several months and required analysis of the political, social and economic processes within the former Soviet republics and study of the various documents and agreements which were drawn up at the many summits and other meetings of CIS members. Only then did I start to draft a programme for the strengthening of stability and security in the entire post-Soviet territory and for the socio-economic modernisation of the new states on a new integrationist platform. Thus was born the project to create the Euro-Asian Union (EAU).

In principle, its basis should be the former Soviet republics or, at least a part of them. This was fully feasible insofar as these countries have acquired over centuries a strong potential to unite with one another; Eurasia has always been an important reality in the lives of their peoples.

The project envisages that an absolute condition of membership of the EAU should be respect of intergovernmental agreements, mutual recognition of the state-political institutions of the member states, territorial integrity and inviolability of borders, a renunciation of any form of pressure in inter-state relations and an end to any military activity between them.

Besides that, I proposed four areas of co-operation: the economy, the humanitarian sphere, defence and ecology. I considered and still consider these to be our main priorities. The more we work together in trying to solve these problems, the quicker we will enjoy success.

The creation of a common economic 'space' would greatly improve what has already been the relatively fast progress which most of the former Soviet republics have made in transforming their economies along market-oriented lines. This is a basic axiom with which it would be difficult for anyone to disagree. However, creation of such a space will remain just talk if we do not see some kind of concrete mechanism. I include in my project the proposal to create certain concrete structures, such as commissions on the economy, on energy resources, intergovernmental financial-industrial groups and joint ventures, and funds for economic and technical co-operation and inter-governmental arbitrage. The creation of such institutions can make it much easier to solve problems which seem virtually insoluble for countries working on their own.

No less important is the project's emphasis on our humanitarian inheritance. The enormous achievements of our science, culture and education systems, created by all of us, were divided up between the independent states and much was lost in the process. For this reason, the aim is also to re-create a single 'space' for the flow of information, science, education and culture which would intensify the dialogue between our peoples in all areas of humanitarian activity.

Another of the key problems which the newly-independent states must resolve is the guarantee of their national security and territorial integrity. After the collapse of the Soviet Union, several areas within it rapidly turned into zones of instability not only because of internal conflicts but also because of deliberate interference from outsiders. Members of the EAU would do much to improve their own security if they decided to tackle such problems together in a mutually acceptable manner.

Fourthly, there is the question of ecological security, which has still not been solved by the CIS countries. This is an especially pressing problem for us, as a result, in particular, of the nuclear and other military tests carried out in Kazakhstan which had such a disastrous effect on our environment. The destruction of the ecological balance in many regions of the former Soviet Union is assuming a growing and increasingly threatening character. It is difficult for individual countries to deal with such problems on their own, not only because of the huge resources that are required but also because many of the problems, such as the drying-up of the Aral Sea, span national borders.

Last, but not least, we must think of the simple living requirements of the people – their freedom of movement, their contact with friends and relatives, and their right to choose where they live and work. These are far from minor problems; indeed, they are far more important than the ambitions of political leaders or the never-ending battle to win votes.

I spoke for the first time about the need to create a new body to strive for integration on the territory of the former Soviet Union not at home but abroad, in early spring 1994, when I was invited to give a speech at the Royal Institute of International Affairs in London while I was on an official visit to Britain. I set out the proposal in more detail in March of the same year during another speech, this time at Moscow University. The choice of venue was deliberate; the audience was full of members of Russia's intellectual élite and I was keen to see how they would react to what I was proposing.

A majority of those present immediately spoke out in support of the project. They, like no one else, understood about the poor state of science and culture in the former Soviet Union and realised that the creation of such an Euro-Asian Union could do much to remedy the situation. But after the speech, Viktor Sadovnichesky, the university's rector, said to me:

'You know that there will be many opponents of your initiative.'

'What makes you think that?' I asked.

'Because it will knock the wind out of the sails of all the windbags and the other lazy people who have done well for themselves,' he retorted.

I discovered the true meaning of his words later when some newspapers began to print articles in which they kicked up a storm about my proposals. My opponents claimed that creation of the EAU would deprive countries of their newly-won sovereignty and bring about a return to the bad old days of empire.

This was a complete misunderstanding of my position. I had not once called for a restoration of the Soviet Union. Our country's independence had become a reality, no one could turn the clock back. If we take the example of the European Union, a central principle has always been respect for national sovereignty. What was to stop us doing the same thing if we decided to set up this Euro-Asian Union?

The idea of creating the EAU is in no way in conflict with the CIS. On the contrary, I never lose the opportunity to stress that the potential of the CIS is still far from exhausted. However paradoxical it may seem, the countries of the EU have still not yet reached the degree of integration which we have among the former Soviet states. Unlike Western Europe, we already have a system of economic, industrial and cultural ties which has been built up over decades. The EU countries are working gradually towards common technological standards; we had them already. Unlike the EU and their army of translators and interpreters, we also have a common language, acceptable to all, in which to conduct our meetings: Russian.

In general, the criticisms of the EAU were way off the mark. Gradually, people began to come out in favour of such an idea in speeches and newspaper articles. Andrei Kozyrev, who was at that time Russian Foreign Minister, said that his country was prepared to hold talks on the question of creating such a Eurasian Union, but only 'after concrete decisions by the parliamentary and political leadership'. It won support from other prominent Russian politicians such as Grigory Yavlinksy, leader of the liberal Yabloko group, and Sergei Shakhrai, head of the Party of Russian Unity and Consent. Although the discussion often provoked heated debate and degenerated into bitter personal disputes, I was not unduly concerned; the most important thing was that our project seemed to have some chance of being realised.

As part of the process of creating the EAU we proposed a variety of very flexible forms and methods of integration, both on a bilateral and multilateral basis. It is important to leave individual states free to decide how quickly – and to what extent – they integrate with their neighbours. The criteria should be objective factors such as the speed of economic transformation, the depth of political reform and the existence – or lack – of the appropriate legal basis. It is understandable that not all members of the CIS are ready for the fullest degree of integration. Nevertheless, I believe that those which are ready will not miss the chance.

And this is precisely what has happened. Initially, what could be described as the western segment of integration was formed, incorporating Russia, Belarus and Kazakhstan. Parallel to this in the East was a second segment grouping Kazakhstan, Uzbekistan and Kyrgyzstan. This first attempt to integrate around two poles acted as a kind of trial balloon. Its results fully confirmed the belief that the common history of our countries dictates that we should live and work together.

The next step to strengthen co-operation of the post-Soviet states was the treaty between Belarus, Kazakhstan, Kyrgyzstan and Russia on deepening integration in the economic and cultural spheres. The Russian Federation and Belarus went yet one step further in spring 1996 in signing a treaty creating a Community of Sovereign States.

As a result, we are able to watch what is turning into an inevitable process – the realisation of the Eurasian project. We now have some new supra-national agencies, such as an EAU Inter-State Executive Committee, which is to be a standing executive and supervisory body. We are optimistic that this committee will be granted observer status by a number of major international organisations. My vision has also won support from many political leaders in Russia, elsewhere in the CIS and beyond.

We politicians of the post-Soviet period have the responsibility of transforming our countries into democratic and civilised societies. Integration of our countries is going to be an imperative of the twenty-first century, but we should start tackling it now. What is the point of leaving these problems unsolved for our children and our grandchildren?

It will be the happiest day of my life when I will at last be able to pick up the stones which were scattered in the parable. In the meantime, I will continue working towards ensuring that this day comes soon.

INDEX OF NAMES